Lost Souls

A Cry to Recapture What is Disappearing
from American Education

Tammi Ann Lawrence

B'S HIVE PUBLISHING
Battle Creek, Michigan

With thanks...

To Tom, Andrew and Megan for their endless love, patience and support through all of my soul searching.

and...

To Jock McCrumb, my mentor, friend and a true soul mate, for the inspiration and regular reminders to believe in myself.

———————

TABLE OF CONTENTS

PREFACE

It may or may not be important for readers of this book to know the context from which I write. I, however, am one of those people that needs to know the "why's" of something and for that reason, it seemed important to provide a small amount of information as to how I came to write this book.

As an assistant principal in a mid-sized high school in Michigan, I have spent the past number of years working with children who were struggling in school and often struggling in other aspects of their lives as well. I often struggled myself with the mounting frustration that came as I found myself incapable of determining ways to help these students succeed both academically and socially within that one area where I thought I had some small measure of control--the school. While their failure in the school setting was one concern, I often found myself feeling a combination of what could only be called sorrow and rage as I watched children not only become involved in non-productive behaviors, but also attempt and succeed in self-destructive ones.

It was perhaps a year ago now that I was slowly drawn into a fascination and understanding of the soul; of it's value and meaning to us as humans; and of its manner of functioning and making its state of health known to us. Through reading and research it became clear to me that it was within the soul and through the soul that all those facets that make us truly human and provide us with character, emotions and wisdom were developed and nurtured. Coupled with this came a dawning awareness that unless the soul itself was developed and nurtured, the potential for any human to develop strength in these areas was severely curtailed.

One thing led to another as I continued my pursuit of understanding the soul until such time as I experienced one of those wonderful "Ah-hah!" moments, and it suddenly became very clear that the most soulful members of our world were, without question, the youngest members of our society--the children. Their simple wisdom, easy joy, love of creating and playing, and their inherent trust in both themselves and the world around them were obvious signs of what I would define as soulfulness. Almost without exception, we speak to the adult enjoyment that comes through watching the innocence of childhood and the value of that time of life.

Yet as I looked around, I also recognized with painful clarity that we have come to a point in time when the value of childhood is being eradicated with an awful determination. All around, the world is speedily moving our children away from the natural things of childhood. Whether in news stories of abused and neglected children or in glitzy advertising, television shows and movies that promote ever-earlier adulthood, the standard time for childhood is being shortened. As this occurs in the world around us, we are also witnessing an increasing number of children who display adult behaviors that we know are detrimental to them and to society; growing leagues of children who are angry and destructive; and a tremendous rise in youth who are withdrawing from the world around them. As our world has become determined to shorten the time for childhood, this pursuit has meant less time for a full development of the souls of our children and, as a consequence, less time for the connected growth in their character, wisdom and emotional health and well-being.

While all this knowledge seemed to come crashing into my consciousness, I was struck by the fact that I was also seeing an educational system that was following the societal trend and that was speedily moving students away from "soulful" pursuits and into ones that have clear steps, processes and answers--in short, ones that might make them better able to fit into the societal picture of what makes a person successful, at least by adult standards. In this system, we train students in those things that enable them to function in the increasingly technological work place. Certainly, I won't discount this entirely. Yet what has been lost is any sort of balance between this and those things that encourage the development of the soul, namely course work and activities that encourage creativity, intuitive thought, self-reliance, beauty, simplicity and recognition of the cyclical pattern found in nature. And as this occurs, our children become less complete--less whole--and more and more of them drop out, physically, mentally or emotionally, from the school setting. Their needs are not being met.

I find myself now, compelled to write a book that reminds both education and society in general that there is a strong need to return to educating the "whole child", with the understanding that this includes both areas of intellectual and soul development. To work towards training them for the primary function of fitting into the economic machinery of the society is well-intended, yet is causing grave harm. We see the results of this in the growing number of teenage pregnancies, in the increase in drug and alcohol use, and in the rise in violence and other forms of dysfunction. While we recognize these as realities, we have also come to blame these on a variety of other, more complex issues, rather than simply realizing that as we deny our children and our students the access to soulful pursuits, we deny them the chance to become not only effective, but equally important, happy individuals as well. In doing so, we have set up the most vicious of circles wherein the unhappiness and dissatisfaction leads to dysfunctional behavior which results in further unhappiness and dissatisfaction. It is a circle that our society has a strong need to break.

This book then is my way of addressing the grief that I have felt as I've watched not only society but also education gradually eradicate anything that might foster soul for our students. I recognize that what follows in the succeeding pages is diametrically opposed to the current thoughts and trends regarding how to best educate our students. I also realize that it is time for there to be a voice that verbalizes what others may be thinking, though they may not be comfortable with the phraseology and definitions regarding the soul that will be found here. Regardless, even those who are comfortable with the current status quo in education yet read what follows with an open mind will see that there is logic and sound reasoning for what is here and what is recommended. It is my deepest hope that then there will be an increase in the number of us who call for a balance in educating our students for both success in our economic world and in the soulful realm as well.

INTRODUCTION

F rom the late 1950's and early 1960's when the nation lived in fear of falling behind the Russians in the space race, to the 1980's and *A Nation at Risk*, focus in American society and education narrowed steadily toward a concentrated push towards preparing our young people for the world that was being created, with a primary emphasis on what we knew would be necessary work-place skills, namely in the areas of math, science and technology. We watched the world's technological progress during this time with awe and perhaps a bit of dread, and believed, with the best of intentions, that it was imperative for education to prepare students for this world which increasingly demanded them to be well-skilled in these areas.

Even when the fears of Sputnik had passed and even after most of the furor over *A Nation at Risk* had died down, American education was terrorized by another fear that caused a redoubling of efforts in educating students in math, science and technology: the concern that we were falling behind other countries, such as Japan, in turning out students prepared to meet the demands of the 21st Century. This fear again fueled the belief that the best that we could do for American youth was to be more rigorous in our demands of them in math, science and technology; to require more course work and credits in these areas; and to turn out students prepared to compete in a global marketplace where these skills are more and more of a necessity. And this we have done.

There is an axiom that cites that any time you have an increased emphasis in one area, there is invariably a correlational decrease in another area. In terms of the education and well-being of American youth, there are a number of concepts which fall under this truism that will be explored in the following pages. First, with the increased demands for course work in the areas of math, science and technology, it follows that there would have to be a decrease in another area. This has traditionally been in the non-academic areas covering creative human endeavors, such as music, theater, fine arts, poetry and creative writing. Even in schools where there is a strong tradition in these areas, it is unlikely to find a commitment to them in terms of graduation requirements. In schools where there is a fine or performing arts credit needed for graduation, it is likely that this can be avoided through alternate selections, such as vocational or practical arts, or even foreign language, any of which may meet the requirement in this area. Worse, those who work with the children in the educational setting are often so focused on preparing students well for the world of work, they encourage students towards the more academic selections, truly believing that the others can be attained either through extra-curriculars or through the home. Arts educators often bemoan this as well as the fact that any time there is a money crunch felt by the schools, the creative areas are those seen as most dispensable and the most logical to curtail, and in these economic times, the foothold these have in the schools across our country often seems tenuous at best.

It should be noted that it is not only the fine and performing arts that have suffered, but truly all of those subject areas which require a similar type of thought process, which I define as less logical-sequential and more intuitive-cyclical and therefore creative. The declining emphasis on these types of subjects is predictable as the movement towards math, science, technology and work-place skills increases.

A second premise is that this trend has had devastating consequences on the young people going through the American education system and that these consequences are in turn creating devastating consequences for American society now and into the foreseeable future. The central title of this book, Lost Souls, refers to that which has been forgotten as curricular work in soul-nurturing endeavors has been relegated to the bottom of society's educational priorities. It is through the more creative and intuitive endeavors that a child has an opportunity to reach inside and explore thoughts, ideas, motives and meanings that are of his own creation. Through such activities, the child comes in touch with his soul and discovers his own potentials for thought, belief and strength. If no time is allotted for this and one considers again the axiom that for any increase in one area there will be a decrease in another, the impact on children going through our educational system becomes clear. As a child is subject to increased training and emphasis in these process-oriented areas, and thereby lesser training in the intuitive, creative and soulful realm, the end product is likely an adult conversant in the ways of the working world, but wholly non-conversant with the way his mind works, what he believes, where his true potentials lie and how to tap into his inner strengths--best explained, out of touch with the workings of his soul and the benefits to be had there in terms of that wisdom, character and emotional health and well-being.

Now this concept may seem foreign to some and some may be concerned with bringing up the word "soul" in connection with education since it involves potential religious connotations.

Perhaps then, a definition of what is meant here by "soul" is in order. A simple definition, if one is possible, cites the soul as an entity responsible for animating a body's existence. Religious definitions and explanations point to the soul's survival following the body's death and connect it therefore to faith and spirituality. In addition to these and more for the purpose of this writing, the soul refers to that part of a person through which all creative thoughts and ideas flow. It may be defined as the conscience of a person, and therefore is the area of the human being that has the "key" to right and wrong. C.G. Jung referred to the soul as the "unconscious"; that is an area that is not known "consciously", but none the less, an entity needing care and concern and exercise if it is to remain healthy. More modern authors define the soul in non-religious terms as well. Robert Sardello links the soul to the "...imaginative possibilities in our nature."[1] In his book, *Care of the Soul*, Thomas Moore writes, " 'Soul' is not a thing, but a quality or a dimension of experiencing life and ourselves. It has to do with depth, value, relatedness, heart and personal substance."[2] And to me, the soul is best defined as the inner voice of a person that can offer us the right answer to the various questions in life, if we are willing to listen to it. When we pair these definitions with the realization that there is less and less not only in the world at large but also within the schools that would foster the development of the soul there is greater understanding as to how many young people are making inappropriate, even disastrous decisions along the path to adulthood. It is equally clear that while many others may be graduating with skills to produce and consume in the society at large, there is mounting evidence that they are less and less likely to find happiness, satisfaction and meaning while doing it.

I noted earlier that those areas currently receiving the greatest emphasis in American schools are those areas which are process-oriented. The subject matter found in the curricular areas of math, science and technology generally has a right and wrong pattern for effective completion. It uses a logical-sequential, or linear, thought pattern. As long as increased school hours are spent in areas requiring this approach, there is less time available for those areas that fall within the creative realm where the work and thought processes are more intuitive-cyclical, more free-flowing and certainly more subjective. Unlike the former, there may well be no clear pattern or procedure for completion; no verifiable right or wrong, which brings us to another premise forming the basis for this writing. The soul craves those things which are, in fact, not necessarily logical, intellectual, or linear-sequential. It is nurtured by things which are not clearly tangible or visible. These things include beauty, creativity, simplicity, love and belonging, self-reliance and faith. It is inclined to the cyclical much like the process that is nature and those curricular subjects noted earlier do little to provide these elements. When society and the schools restrict the expression or devalue the importance of the soul by curtailing our children's access to soul-related pursuits and course work, moving them too rapidly into adult standards of success, we fail to educate to the "whole child" and this has serious repercussions.

The amount of evidence that supports these points and the underlying premise here is staggering. You need only look at the drop out rate, the suicide rate among teenagers and young adults, the increased rate of violent crime among youth, the rise in teenage pregnancy and the use of alcohol, tobacco and other drugs to realize that something is wrong. News reports, studies, and statistics all point to a variety of extraneous reasons for these problems, but little if any focus has been placed on the simple realization that there are rapidly dwindling resources being allocated to help children care for that most necessary part of their being--the soul. To the contrary, if you read the paper, watch the evening news, or attend school board or P.T.A. meetings, you will quickly realize what strength there is behind educating to the intellect of our children at the expense of that other equally important entity.

The following pages are devoted to encouraging others to recognize that we have lost any sense of balance, not only in the world at large but also in the world of education. As an idealist, I'll admit that I have hopes of seeing our world and society return to emphasizing and valuing the importance of childhood and the natural, soul-nurturing activities inherent there. The realist in me, however, recognizes that to modify a society-wide trend is a task of Herculean proportions. Yet it doesn't seem unrealistic to believe that there is hope in reminding both society and education that, at least within the schools of America, there can be a blend between preparing our children for the economic world they will enter and providing for the needs of their souls. The hope here is for recognition and realization that one doesn't have to lose out over the other and that it is not too late to find the "lost souls" in American education.

PART I

Losing Soul in Our World and the Schools

For as much emphasis as there is in the world around us on what ails us as a society, I am regularly struck by how little focus is given to the fact that our nation and the world at large has sought to educate its inhabitants away from a connection to their souls. In part because the ills of society generally make themselves known among the students with whom I regularly interact and also because of the common sense understanding one can get through reading and research on the soul, it only seemed right to work towards providing an understanding of the importance of the soul to those who impact the lives of the children who are and will be our future.

To me, it not only made sense, it also fit in with the idea that the soul was in need of simplicity. As we look at societal problems, we are likely to blame some very complex issues--dysfunctional homes, a disappearing middle class, the impact of television and other media, drug and alcohol abuse--the list is lengthy. Yet all these seem nothing more than symptoms of what can occur when the souls of a populace are disregarded as entities of value and lose out on the nurturing and exercise that they need. The severity of our societal problems, particularly among our youth, is not dismissed as being unimportant here, but the mission of what follows is to offer a rarely-considered perspective. Our history over the past decades has been one that has moved away from the recognition of and opportunities for those things that once nurtured our souls. As the saying goes, those who don't learn from history are doomed to repeat it. To modify this saying here, it might be better put that if we don't come to an understanding as to how we have moved our society and our children away from a connection with their souls, we won't be necessarily repeating history, but we will indeed be continuing on the road of problems and dysfunction that we currently find ourselves traveling.

It is to this end that the next chapters are devoted. Understanding our history and how we have moved away from our souls and looking at the resulting consequences is an important part of attempting to recapture that which is disappearing from American education.

CHAPTER 1

Towards an Understanding

The world we live in is an interesting place and the humans that inhabit it are one of the biggest fascinations. If you take a moment to essentially remove yourself mentally from the role of participant in the game of life and observe the world objectively, taking in the whole picture, things become frighteningly clear. You see a place where change and progress are the name of the game. The rules of this game have been modified over time so that what has come to mean individual and societal success are those things that cast a person in a role where he functions as an efficient part of the economic machinery found in that world. Material wealth, financial success, technological expertise, ability to make use of the logical and practical and other similar values are the measure by which the participants are judged. In looking at this, it seems as well that those who are cast as the "losers" in this game are those people who cannot or who do not wish to function solely as part of the machinery and who may strike out on different paths, playing by different rules and measuring their success by different standards.

There have always been those people who did not fit into the standard of success of their time. In the early 1800's when Ralph Waldo Emerson wrote his essay entitled "Self-Reliance", he noted that society quickly identified who the "losers" were. "For non-conformity, the world whips you with displeasure."[1] he wrote, pointing out that the world had specific means for measuring the success and value of individuals and those means included how well they fit into the world around them--how well they could conform to the expectations of the society they inhabited.

As our technological progress has developed and thrived and as we have moved quickly into today's "information age", we are increasingly beset by visions of what the world considers appropriate conformity to the standards of "winning" in the game of life. Televisions relay images of what we need to be, have and do in order to be a success. Magazine advertisements create vivid pictures of what the world's winners look like. The news media bring stories into our homes of the powerful and important and then offer us a contrast by showing the opposite ends of the spectrum in those who are poor, downtrodden and dysfunctional; it almost seems a warning. And those of us who make our living in education are faced with children who have grown up with these images and who have been educated prior to their arrival at school to believe that material success is what it takes to be a winner in this world.

While there may not be anything inherently wrong in this, there is something that is lacking and which has, over time, been de-emphasized and almost lost to the world. That is the recognition that the true winners in this world are those who are well-balanced; those who have blended the ability to function successfully in the world around them without losing touch with their souls. Yet there is very little in the world we live in that speaks to any need to be balanced. There may be some small recognition of this, but over the past few decades in particular, it has been pushed out of focus. For some, the lack of focus is not a problem and they instinctively balance material well-being with the well-being of their soul. For others, particularly our children who are being strongly educated and influenced by the world around them, the diminished focus on balancing and blending these two needs is, as noted in the introduction, having damaging and far-reaching consequences.

UNDERSTANDING THE SOUL

Before the impact of this lack of balance is explored in any more depth, the whole concept of soul must be examined. Consider for a moment the world around you. Any of us can reflect on the movement of our lives and those things so prevalent in the day to day process of living. The times we live in are incredibly busy. Our lives are fast-paced; often hectic. We are beset by information that bombards us from every side. We are involved in a myriad of activities through work and friendships. Our children participate in any number of activities designed to make sure that they are "well-rounded". And the constant refrain you will hear from those around you as well as from your own mouth is that there "just isn't enough time in the day". All this is easily verified and as we live through this time, these things that keep us constantly on the move, overly busy and regularly attempting to keep up with the status quo are precisely those things that prevent us from coming or remaining in touch with our souls. So as to simplify definitions here, I refer to all these things as "outside voices" which have, over the course of history, become so loud and clear that they have drowned out our "inner voices", the voices of our souls.

What is the soul? Never clearly defined by religion, philosophy or psychology, perhaps the simplest and most easily understood definition names the soul as that inner voice of man. It is a voice that can be heard when we have the time to be quiet, to reflect, and to meditate without the pressure and volume of those outside voices and is, therefore, a voice that our world makes more and more difficult to be heard.

The soul is the voice that tells us what is right and wrong; the voice that gives us direction in life and can point out the paths we should take. It is a voice that has a wealth of knowledge. C.G. Jung reflected in an essay written in 1933 that the soul, or as he referred to it, the unconscious, was not to be disregarded. "A high regard for the unconscious psyche as a source of knowledge is by no means such a delusion as our Western rationalism likes to suppose," he wrote. "We are inclined to presume that, in the last resort, all knowledge comes from without. Yet today we know for certain that the unconscious contains contents which would mean an immeasurable increase in knowledge if they could only be made conscious."[2] The world as it is, however, prevents us from making this knowledge available as those inner voices that would deliver it to us are drowned out and devalued by the volume of the world and, if it does get past the outside voices, it is disregarded because it is not explainable through the scientific, logical means that we have been taught to trust.

As well, it is the soul that allows us to be human and to experience the gamut of emotions so unique to our species. The soul allows us the highs of love, joy, happiness and beauty as well as the lows of loss, grief, despair and pain. Through the soul we feel both pride and shame, innocence and guilt. Name your emotion, it is through these feelings that the soul makes its presence known and allows us to be more than just a "being"; it allows us our humanity. Without a well-nurtured, healthy connection with the soul, the resultant consequence is a human without the ability to feel all those emotions; a human who displays a frightening lack of affect; a human who can have horrifying effects on the people and world around him.

Perhaps due to the difficulty in defining, locating and

labeling, and certainly due to the inability to prove definitive existence to the satisfaction of scientists and scholars, belief in the soul and recognition of its value to the human experience has been lost over time. A retrospective on history that tracks human progress through the various ages illustrates this with startling clarity. From the beginning of time through to the industrial age, there has been an ever decreasing emphasis on those things outside the realm of human consciousness and experience. Since the soul falls well outside this area, over time it has been discarded as something of value and has become more of a theoretical or religious concept. Tied into this is the trend towards reliance on the scientific and the logical, so that today, thanks in part to the abundance of scientific knowledge and understanding, anything that can not be quantified, observed or measured is dismissed. And so, outside of churches and religion, the soul is not often taken as a serious concept.

Someone well-versed in science and rational and logical patterns of thinking may easily dismiss the importance of all the foregoing, believing fully that human society is functioning quite nicely without placing any strong emphasis on the soul. We can all point with pride to our progress in many areas, illustrating how effectively our technological and scientific improvements have allowed us to eradicate a variety of problems previously faced by human society. The gains in these areas can be credited with the elimination of a number of diseases, with our ability to access information with incredible speed, with our ability to travel vast distances in a shorter and shorter period of time, with our increasing understanding of how the universe is made up or any other of the variety of wonders in the modern age.

The value of these can't be disputed, yet some of the other things that have come part and parcel with these technological gains should be taken into account as well. With this progress, human society has moved increasingly away from any faith in things that are not visible or tangible to a reliance almost solely on things that can be understood through logical, scientific means. The society spends billions of dollars in research and studies that seek to offer logical explanations for all of the mysteries of our world, meeting with some degree of success. Coupled with this change has been the increase in the speed in which we find ourselves operating. There are more and more activities in which to be engaged; there is a wealth of information to be processed; there are increasing opportunities to be considered and there are louder, more powerful voices sending information as to what you should do and have to be successful. No matter who you are or where you might be in life, all around you are things outside yourself, seemingly logical and rational, that provide you with answers as to who you are, what you should be, how you should think, what you should believe, and why you should place your trust in their wisdom and information.

A connection is quite easily established, however, between these facts of life and the fact that this trend away from balance between the scientific and intellectual and the intuitive and soulful has come with a hefty price tag. The increase in this movement correlates closely with the decrease in societal health and happiness. This is evidenced by an upswing in escapism, through drug and alcohol abuse, through blaming others for problems, and through violence and suicide. It is seen as the number of divorces increase, with an increase in the number of children in single-parent homes. Among our youth, the rate of teen pregnancy shocks and saddens us; we are horrified by the children who assault and murder with little emotion; we watch the rise in drug use with fear. Simply stated, all of these illustrate what occurs when people seek to find something outside themselves to make them happy and to alleviate the pain felt through loss of touch with the soul. Anyone who can operate with a measure of reason and logic will realize that the future includes more of the same. With the increased reliance on those outside voices and the corresponding decrease in trust of the inner ones of soul, you realize that more and more of our world's inhabitants may be functioning as a reasonable part of the society's machinery, but that they are suffering a growing dissatisfaction and dysfunction in doing so.

The unhappiness that comes intertwined with the loss of connection to the soul is a logical outgrowth of the world we live in. As we are kept too busy and too rushed and as we rely on things outside of ourselves for happiness, it is easy to dismiss those things that would provide for exercise and nurturing of the soul. The soul gains strength through quiet times, opportunities to be creative, moments to spend in the beauty and quiet of the natural world and a measure of self-reliance as opposed to conformity to specified standards. There is so little in the world that speaks to or promotes such things, that it is quite easy to dismiss that they are, indeed, not only important, but vital to our ability to be balanced and whole, and if we are not, unhappiness and dissatisfaction is invariably the result.

A CASE FOR BALANCE

It should not be assumed that every human who inhabits the planet is suffering from a malaise associated with lack of soul. There are numerous individuals who live their lives as effectively functioning humans and who recognize the value, purpose and meaning of their lives. While many of these may not credit their state of mental health and their happiness to the well-being and strength of their soul, they will probably at least define their lives as being "balanced". For these people, they function well in the home, the work place, or other areas they find themselves in. They are efficient, productive, skilled and capable. In addition to the ability to function effectively in the world around them, they have also maintained a solid grounding in those things that nurture the soul. They may find opportunities to be creative through music or artistic endeavors; they may take time to shut off the volume of the world around them and enjoy moments of quiet solitude. They relish the opportunities for excursions into natural settings, or to plant gardens and flowers. They trust themselves and their natural wisdom and intuition enough to carefully evaluate those outside voices and determine the true merit of what is being said, taught or encouraged. They establish and maintain bonds of love and belonging with their friends and their families. These people are well-balanced and move gracefully between heeding the voices of the world and the voice of their soul. This balance provides for general happiness and satisfaction, and they are capable of avoiding any overwhelming tendency to seek things outside of themselves to be happy.

But these people and the world they inhabit are increasingly affected by those who have lost the connection to soul. Robert Sardello notes that there is, "...a tremendous void of love, and thus of soul in the world. This void does not remain empty but is taken up primarily by scientific, technological, and economic materialism, which would try to make a world full of substitutes for love and soul."[3] Yet those substitutes which are always outside of ourselves and often difficult and expensive to have and maintain lead to a tremendous neglect of the soul. Thomas Moore identifies the problems associated with this. "When the soul is neglected, it doesn't just go away; it appears symptomatically in obsessions, addictions, violence and loss of meaning."[4] Since our world and our society are undeniably interdependent, what affects one affects the whole, so that as we witness the increase in the numbers of individuals, organizations and situations where the soul is neglected and denied, it is hard for people to be individually content that they still have a soul connection.   The world we all inhabit is too profoundly impacted by those who do not.

To understand this in more concrete terms, all you need to do is read an evening newspaper or watch a typical news program. You will hear about urban areas where graffiti, decay, violence and hopelessness are the norm. You will listen to discussions of increasing numbers of police being hired and trained to fight the growing rate of crime. Stories will be presented illustrating how industries have polluted the environment, dumping toxic waste into rivers, streams and oceans so as to save dollars. You will learn how more tax dollars are being spent to build prisons with less spent on education. You can watch in disbelief as reports are made as to the new and more deadly weapons that are falling into the hands of governments and private individuals. You may cringe in horror at the stories of young people who wound or kill others, and display no remorse, but rather the lack of affect that comes through the distancing from soul. It is no wonder that after being exposed to all this, your complacency and self-assurance that you are in touch with your soul fades. In looking at the big picture, it is clear that the old adage is true: No man is an island. The lack of soul in the world today and the movement away from balance is having profound consequences on all of us.

THOSE WITH AND THOSE
WITHOUT THE SOUL CONNECTION

So why is it that there are many people who are in touch with their soul and so many who are not? What creates the difference? Who are those who get and maintain the connection and who are the ones who either never connect with the soul or lose touch with it somewhere along life's path? A simplistic explanation to begin with may be offered up in terms of religious faith. Churches offer that those who exercise a solid faith in God may be less prone to problems such as Moore identifies and, like Moore, religions stress the value and importance of the soul as an entity. Yet even in churches, the soul often remains an ineffectively defined concept and for that reason alone remains relegated to the tenets of religious organizations. Unfortunately, the simple wisdom to "have faith" is lost on much of the world today. As we have moved further and further from reliance on simple faith--believing without seeing--and traveled to where we are now, where our trust is placed in the observable, measurable and tangible, the religions and the faith that we had once so valued have lost significance. This movement away from simple faith has been a long time in the making. Carl Jung wrote in 1932 of the historical trend. "We are now reaping the fruit of nineteenth-century education. Throughout that period, the Church preached to young people the merit of blind faith, while the universities inculcated an intellectual rationalism, with the result that today we plead in vain whether for faith or reason. Tired of this warfare of opinions, the modern man wishes to find out for himself how things are."[5]

It does seem that the result of our growing scientific and technological knowledge there has been a correlational decrease in our belief in things of faith, including the soul. It is equally true that the people who inhabit the world more and more indicate a desire to find out for themselves how things are, yet the opportunities to do this are severely limited by the overwhelming amount of information that is constantly vying for our attention, in many cases totally preventing our ability to hear, let alone trust, the instinctive, intuitive wisdom that arises from the soul. The fortunate among us--those cited earlier as being well-balanced--seem to have an inherent or acquired ability to find a middle ground between faith or soulfulness, and intellectual or scientific reasoning. These are those people who function in society, create meaning in their lives and find satisfaction in their work and in their world.

It is fairly safe to assume while this ability to find a balance, whether inherent or acquired, is one that requires at least some degree of effort to maintain. In order to do so, a person must be capable of carefully considering that deluge of information coming on so strong from those outside voices and then basing decisions on an evaluation that takes into consideration both the information of the world and the wisdom of the soul. Because such decisions have invariably good results, to evaluate in such a manner and then act accordingly creates a sense of self-reliance and self-trust that perpetuates itself in future decision-making opportunities.

For others, the ability to blend or balance faith with reason is a struggle. These people, who are without firm conviction are as rudderless ships, moving with and directed by whatever societal wind blows the strongest. These winds are those outside voices: the external stimuli, information and influences that buffet all humans from every side. During our current period of history, these winds are powerful ones indeed. They include media portrayals of violence and promiscuity as the norm; news accounts of war, pestilence, poverty and crime to the virtual exclusion of societal good; advertising that promises happiness, love, wealth and success--for the price of a given product; work environments that reward those who place the organization over self; a legal system that fosters lack of individual responsibility, and a host of changing norms that sanction a variety of "personal freedoms". How confusing for the directionless in our world! As these voices grow in volume, there is little wonder that those who are without a well-grounded connection to their soul become confused, disoriented and go astray. Their ability to hear the inner voice of the soul has atrophied, and since all humans need direction, they follow those of the societal winds, the outside voices of this world.

The unfortunate outcome of this tendency is for those who are so off-balance and so out of touch with their soul is a reliance on things outside themselves for happiness and meaning. The intuitive wisdom that would advise them that continually chasing expensive or unattainable material possessions will not lead to long-term satisfaction is not allowed to be heard. Instead, those outside voices are able to sell reliance on those material things for happiness, security and a sense of self. For those without a solid grounding in themselves--in their soul--this message is readily bought and paid for, but the price for both the individual and the world is high. It is a price that demands investment of time, money or one's very being in something which promises gratification. Yet when the newness or novelty wears off, when the time devoted leads to unbearable stress or when life seems to have become a self-defeating treadmill, the shopping trip for a different source of satisfaction begins anew, thus setting up a vicious circle. In terms of the economics of the society, this is a valuable circle which keeps full the coffers of businesses, attorneys, physicians, psychiatrists and even churches. As long as people seek to "buy" their sense of self-worth, the world as we know it, a huge economic enterprise, can continue.

If you recognize the truth in this, you may question why such a vicious circle is allowed to continue and to understand this, you can simply consider how we have educated the inhabitants of this world. Take a hypothetical case of a child who is educated from the earliest part of his existence that "two plus two equals three". As long as the most powerful voices in his life, often the media or others who have been educated by it, inculcate him with the belief that "two plus two equals three" and constantly reinforce this as knowledge and truth, even his intuitive and logical recognition of the inaccuracy will be met with denial. He may come to realize and recognize that the correct answer is "four", but the outside voices that have so powerfully influenced him can make him doubt and deny provable knowledge, and are that much more effective in making him doubt and deny his own wisdom--the voice of his soul.

While this example may be seem extreme, it serves to illustrate what we have created. We have a wonderfully vast array of information sources that have become powerful voices. They have, as noted, taught many people that "two plus two equals three" and these are the same people who believe that their sense of self can be bought for the right price. As they continually pay that price time and time again, their dissatisfaction mounts and their "lost souls" begin to make themselves felt in some very unpleasant ways that influence our society as a whole.

REAPING WHAT HAS BEEN SOWN IN THE WORLD...

That we have come to a point in time where there are so many humans who have a diminished or non-existent connection to the soul is not very difficult to understand. It was noted earlier that you could run through a retrospective on history through the various ages of humankind and see an ever-increasing reliance on those things that could be explained through the   logical and scientific, with a correlational decrease in reliance on faith and things unseen. For the purposes here however, we need only review the past forty to fifty years of history to get a clear picture as to how we have so effectively dissuaded our population away from a connection with the soul.

The movement away from a balance between faith and intellect had been a long time in the making when the Twentieth Century reached its mid-point. With the emergence of the Soviet Union as a scientific and technological power following the launching of Sputnik in 1957, this movement became more rapid and pronounced. All of a sudden, the United States realized that it was not the world leader in space technology and the government began to provide money to encourage development in this and other related areas. The emphasis and money paid off and on May 5, 1961, when Freedom 7 was launched, the United States was on the track toward worldwide preeminence in space technology and related disciplines that it had so desired.

The technological progress accelerated rapidly during this time and great strides were made in a host of areas, perhaps none so powerful as the growth and development of the electronic media. During the first two-thirds of the Twentieth Century, the world moved from communicating via the written word or telegraph to being able to broadcast pictures and sound vast distances to literally millions of people. The power of the electronic media was clear and it did not take long for American businesses and politicians to take full advantage of that power to convince people of what they should have and how they should think. With this came an increased reliance within the society to use this medium as an educational tool. There was no need to read a lengthy newspaper when the electronic media could feed you a version of the same story in a shorter and perhaps more entertaining form. There was decreasing need to communicate orally with those around you when there was so much entertainment to be had with the television in your living room. There was less incentive to imagine the characters or settings of a well-written story or novel when the television gave you a visual image to rely on. Yet those things, the reading and consideration of a newspaper or book, the oral communication with family and friends, the exercise of the imagination used when reading a novel are precisely the types of things that foster soul, and through the growth in technological progress and prowess, such things were on a rapid decline.

If technological progress meant only a lesser focus on soul-related pursuits, that would be one thing, but there was much more that resulted due to our progress in technology and the resultant reliance on it. As people became more aware of the world around them via this new media, there developed a new focus on what the "norm" was. People were educated effectively as to the new and improved products and gadgets that they should have and what they should be and do in order to function effectively, efficiently and happily in the modern world. The message was so pervasive and so persuasive that it was easy to believe that "everybody" was either "doing it" or "had it" and the desire to obtain these guarantees of happiness increased. Better yet, if the item you wanted had a price out of your range, a thing called credit was now readily available so that you could have your gratification instantly. When the debt on the credit became so great that a single income in the household was not enough, then the traditional stay-at-home mom disappeared into the work force, ready to add her wages to her husband's in order to obtain or maintain the standard of living that they were being educated that everyone should have.

Yet as mothers entered the work force in droves, they met new difficulties, such as caring for their children, preparing meals and taking care of their homes. In a world that functions as an economic machine, however, no need goes unmet. In these situations, children found the television as an entertaining babysitter; fast food restaurants rose to prominence meeting the needs of mothers too tired to cook; and new appliances and gadgets provided for easier home care--but all of these came with more than just a monetary price tag. They also further hindered the ability to be in touch with the soul and its inner voice. Going hand in hand with this movement was that increased pace, that lack of time, and that frenzied rush to keep up with the world that so precludes being in touch with soul. The quiet, reflective times to be introspective disappeared behind the volume of the television; the opportunities to create pleasant meals and family times lost out to the rush to work and keep up; the chances to move out quietly into natural settings decreased and the souls within human society began to rebel against this neglect. Soon, people started to recognize the dissatisfaction they were feeling without knowing why and there was little if anything to define that this discomfort and unhappiness was intertwined with and connected to the diminishing of the soul.

AND IN THE SCHOOLS...

The schools of America are often said to be microcosms of the society at large and certainly in the last 40 to 50 years, this has been true. In part due to America's emergence as a super power following World War I and II and then solidified with the launching of Sputnik, by the late 1950's the fate of American school children had pretty much been sealed in terms of the education that they were to receive. While there had always been a push to educate to the intellect, now it was an obsession. As America feared a loss of that super power status, money was provided to improve what was happening in the schools in terms of math, science and technology education. An example of such funding was found in the National Defense Education Act of 1958, through which money was provided for improvements in the teaching of science, mathematics, technology and foreign language.

Even after the launching of Freedom 7 this emphasis did not diminish and the demand for educating students thoroughly in math, science and technology continued through the 1960's and 1970's. Schools improved and the country experienced economic expansion that made it seem sure that it was on the right track. Yet in 1983, the self-contentment and confidence that the U.S. had surpassed other countries in educating its youth was shattered when Secretary of Education Terrel Bell issued a scathing report entitled "A Nation at Risk: The Imperative for Educational Reform". Truly a fear-inducing document, the opening of the report read, "Our Nation is at risk. Our once unchallenged preeminence in commerce, industry, science and technological innovation is being overtaken by competitors throughout the world. This report is concerned with only one of the many causes and dimensions of the problem, but it is one that under girds American prosperity, security and civility." The report went on to identify that the "...educational foundations of our society are presently being eroded by a rising tide of mediocrity that threatens our very future as a nation and a people."[6] The words of this report struck a national nerve and the trend towards educating students in math, science and technology was further ingrained into the American educational system.

Unfortunately, the short term gains of this trend have led to some very unappealing long term consequences. With the increase in education to the intellectual, there was bound to be a decrease in some other area and course work in soul-nurturing areas--art, music, theater and the like--was the obvious choice. Mirroring the society at large, the schools relegated such course work to the optional, the extra, the "fluff". Students were not only less likely to be encouraged to enroll in such course work, the world at large was quite effectively educating them that it really wasn't necessary and certainly had much less value than being well-skilled in those intellectual areas.

When the changes in family dynamics that intensified during this time are considered in conjunction with the stresses being placed on American education to educate students to be efficient members of the economic community--good workers and consumers--there were serious results in store. As with the adults around them, fewer young people were finding the opportunities to engage in experiences that would nurture their souls, for those things were now less likely in the schools and less likely in the homes as well. And like those adults around them, young people within the schools started displaying the disturbing symptoms that occur when the soul feels neglect. Teenage violence increased. The rate of teenage pregnancy skyrocketed. Dropout rates inched upwards. And the schools themselves reported growing cases of severe discipline problems. Yet no focus was given to the idea that we had taken the balance away from our children. We had dismissed their need to be educated as "whole" human beings, with both intellects and souls, and were reaping the consequences of what we had sown.

As we approach the 21st Century, this pattern has not only remained, but has strengthened and gained momentum. The number of single-parent families is staggering. Child abuse and neglect is common. Parents have less time to spend with their children in meaningful ways, preferring instead to provide for television and video games as the in-home teacher. As this media has been such a strong educator of our young people since birth, they have grown up believing that material goods and possessions are equated with happiness. And greater numbers of children, whether in large cities or small towns are without knowledge of what it is to take the time to simply walk in nature and enjoy the beauty to be found there. All of these things are the antithesis of a soulful life, and the resulting impact has been severe.

In education, the emphasis remains the same as it has for the past forty years, but stronger and with greater momentum as well. The Federal Government's recent push, "Goals 2000", continues to stress the creation of productive workers and citizens through education. Under the category of student achievement, this document states, "All students will leave grades 4, 8, and 12 having demonstrated competency in challenging subject matter including English, mathematics, science, foreign languages, civics and government, economics, arts, history and geography, and every school in America will ensure that all students learn to use their minds well so they may be prepared for responsible citizenship, further learning and productive employment in our nation's modern economy." Another section calls for U.S. Students to be "first in the world in mathematics and science achievement". Even the section on adult literacy and lifelong learning calls for creating productive workers, saying, "Every adult American will be literate and will possess the knowledge and skills necessary to compete in a global economy and exercise the rights and responsibilities of citizenship."[7]

These sound like lofty and worthy goals and you might even call attention to the fact that "arts" is included in the section on student achievement and citizenship, but the fact remains that the predominant theme in the "Goals 2000" document and in education in general today is the push to educate our students in the areas of math, science and technology. Though there may be some recognition that the arts are important, those in education will affirm that what gets money gets the emphasis and attention and currently this is those areas that are, as noted in the introduction, logical and process-oriented, and less likely to foster development of the soul. The concern here centers around the realization that as these things receive strong emphasis, we may do well in ensuring a continued growth in our economic and technological progress, but there is question as to what will diminish as a result of this movement away from educating the "whole child". Further, you have to wonder whether our society can truly thrive when fewer and fewer people have had the opportunity to develop and nurture their souls and as they increase their display of those symptoms intertwined with its neglect.

Educators will verify the foregoing in terms of what is currently being emphasized in American education. They will, if they are honest, testify as well to the trend that is going hand in hand with it, and that is educating students for the work force from the earliest grades. Current initiatives in education such as "school-business partnerships" and "school-to-work" programs are becoming common place, so that schools are not only stressing math, science and technology, but are also encouraging a blending of these into units of study that prepare a student to move from the halls of his or her high school into the work force, whether or not the student has plans to continue on to college or not. In a world such as we live, there is little question as to the worth of this. The question comes when we realize that there was already a heavy emphasis on those things that would encourage a student to become intellectually proficient and to include yet another emphasis that will make them skilled for the work place leaves little if any time in the average student's school day to engage in studies that allow for creativity, introspection and aesthetics. If these are indeed those areas that allow for nurturing and exercising the soul, and if, indeed, this area needs nurturing and exercise for a human to be truly content and happy, as well as to be able to discern between right and wrong, then the problems developing among a rapidly growing number of teenagers seem a logical outgrowth. As more students are discouraged from those soul-nurturing areas due to the curricular requirements of their schools, missing out on the course work that calls for intuitive thought, introspection and is cyclical in nature, and also live in homes devoid of these, their rebellion, or perhaps better stated, the rebellion of their souls, becomes apparent as more of them engage in violence, drug and alcohol abuse, behavioral problems and mental and physical withdrawl from the school setting and often society as well.

CHAPTER 2

Lost Childhood and Lost Souls

Those people who have been in education for any period of time will verify that it seems that whenever society is in a quandary over a given issue, the schools of America are given the task of addressing it. Simply witness the impetus on different areas that schools must address: sex education, AIDS awareness, multi-cultural education, drug education, parenting classes for pregnant teens and then day-care for their children, immunization updates, gender equity, and a host of others. For this reason, the idea that now there should be something else to fall under schools' lists of duties, especially something as nebulous as "nurturing soul", may strike many as ludicrous. Yet the schools not only have ample opportunity to foster soul without any major curricular or structural adjustments but also have a stake in encouraging and nurturing the souls within their student bodies. So perhaps it is first important to consider why there is a strong need for soul-related pursuits within the schools.

WHERE HAVE ALL THE CHILDREN GONE?

At the beginning of each school year, as children make their way back to school, parents tend to breathe a collective sigh of both relief and sadness. There is some relief to know that our children are back in the well-educated hands of those who are paid to teach and nurture their learning. There is sadness in realizing with each passing year that our children are growing up and into a world for which they need to be well prepared. Yet as we send them off into those schools, there may also be some fear, for as those schools truly mirror the society around them, they are reflecting their desire to turn their students into efficient members of that world, and in the process, are mirroring the societal trend that encourages them to grow up too fast.

That there is what amounts to a societal assault on childhood is not difficult to verify. There is simply too much evidence found on television, in news programs and magazines. We watch our youth in the malls and on our streets and comment how much more grown-up they are these days as opposed to a decade or so ago, and in many ways this saddens us. Yet this is without question part and parcel of the world they have been educated by. What is even more discouraging is that what should be the last bastions in defense of childhood, the schools, are more and more surrendering their mission to protect childhood and are joining forces with the world at large that seems to seek to destroy it.

The time allowed for childhood and the health and well-being of the soul are closely interrelated. As we step back and watch small children, we will find that the things that they most naturally pursue are those things that nurture the soul. They are naturally creative, enjoying finger painting, coloring, making up stories or any other activity that calls upon their imagination. They prefer the simple to the complex, opting often for the box as opposed to the expensive and elaborate toy that might have been inside. These, our youngest, display an inherent desire to love and be loved, as well as a trust in both themselves and those around them. It is only as they move into adolescence and adulthood that the full impact of the education that the world will have upon them makes itself known, but, given enough time to be children and explore the natural things of childhood, the soul develops strength to maintain its well-being against the assault of those outside voices.

In our world today, there is less and less time allotted for childhood. In a simple but enlightening book, *The Te of Piglet*, author Benjamin Hoff follows up a previous book, *The Tao of Pooh*, in explaining the principles of Taoism, all of which are truly soul-related. "Mentally, emotionally and physically, the human being is designed for a long childhood, followed by a short adolescence and then adulthood--the state of responsible, self-reliant wholeness." he writes. "What we see children experiencing now, however, is an ever shorter childhood, followed by a premature, prolonged adolescence from which ever fewer seem to be emerging."[1] This last is understandable since in the world at large the trend has been and remains as one in which children are short-changed or rushed through those developmentally appropriate steps in an effort to move them to a point where they are capable of effective functioning. In doing so, however, there is a dismissal as well of that necessary childhood so important to the health of the soul.

Schools are, without exception, staffed by people who are well-meaning, concerned and caring; people who have at least some background in childhood development and psychology, so it is dismaying to watch the schools join in the destruction of childhood. From kindergarten through the twelfth grade, today's educational trends and fads are concerned almost solely with utilizing technology, science, math, integration of subject matter and even career awareness. Where childhood in the schools was once marked by a balance between these and creative play, imagination, beginning interpersonal skill development and enjoyment through simple things like blocks and coloring, it is rapidly becoming a time of computerized learning, lessons and activities of structured and complex proportions and lessened time for imaginative and creative play, and through this the time for childhood of American youth is being systematically stripped from them. It is little wonder that there is so much dissatisfaction among the children in American schools. Yes, the process may serve to create children who are able to function in an increasingly technological world, but there is a question as to whether they can find happiness and satisfaction in either the process or the end result.

Those quite certain that this movement is a beneficial one will contend that without such skills our children will move into the world totally unprepared for what it presents to them. They will, especially if their livelihood is earned through employment in the public schools, expound on the many merits of this new technology and the complexity with which they are burdening children. Why would they do otherwise? In doing so, they perpetuate the myth that the teaching of children is a difficult, demanding, stress-producing career, fully meriting larger salaries than they command. They will further espouse the benefits of year-round schooling for youngsters, though their own contractual year should continue to run for nine or ten months. It should be mentioned that those so personally involved with the education of America's children do not do this with any malicious intent; indeed, it is more likely that they have been so indoctrinated by the outside voices of this world that they truly believe in all that they are saying and all the things that they are doing to create an educational system such as we have today. Well-meaning or non-malicious though it may be, the bottom line is still the irrefutable fact that as we move away from the creativity, the simplicity, the intuitive areas and the opportunities for awareness and appreciation of beauty and move full steam towards the linear, the logical, the complex and the things outside oneself, the more students and young people in general we are finding to exhibit patterns of behavior that illustrate all the things associated with the loss of soul. And in all truth, it is these resultant behaviors that are causing the difficulties and problems that American educators are regularly dealing with. If teaching or administering in today's public schools is demanding, it is not due to the inherent difficulty of the job or the newest demands or trends, but due to the fact that those things that we are incorporating dismiss the simplicity of childhood and soulfulness, and lead to a build up in complexity and stress, not only for the children but for educators as well.

Those who recognize the value of childhood and the soul question the soundness of today's educational attitudes. Thomas Moore writes, "...An eternal question asked about children is how should we educate them? Politicians and educators consider more school days in a year, more science and math, the use of computers and other technology in the classroom, more exams and tests, more certifications for teachers, and less money for art. All of these responses come from the place where we want to make the child into the best adult possible, not in the ancient Greek sense of virtuous and wise, but in the sense of one who is an efficient part of the machinery of society. But on all these counts, soul is neglected. We want to prepare the ego for the struggle of survival, but we overlook the needs of the soul."[2] Likewise, Hoff comments in *The Te of Piglet*, "In response to the declining Test Scores of recent years, the educational system has brought in vastly expensive machines to do the teaching--a sign of trouble if there ever was one. Learn to write from a computer, and so on. (Of course it could have brought in people who knew how to write, or whatever, to teach how to write, or whatever--on a volunteer basis, if necessary. But that would have been too simple, we suppose. Cheating, almost.) Now this costly Teaching Technology is bankrupting the system. So in order to cut costs, the Eeyores are eliminating what they consider unnecessary classes--Art, Creative Writing, Drama, and so on--classes that help students observe, reason and communicate...The Eeyores Educational System sees childhood as a waste of time, a luxury that society cannot afford. It's response to the problems of vanishing childhood is to speed up the process--give the students more information, give it to them at a faster rate, and give it to them sooner. Put children in school at the earliest age possible; load them down with homework; take away their time, their creativity, their play, their power; then plug them into machines. That'll whip them into shape. Well, it'll whip them anyway."[3]

All of this ties into the idea that schools are mirroring the societal trend that strips students of soul-related pursuits, due in large part to the emphasis in our world at large as to what is most valued and valuable, namely educating students to be productive workers and consumers. When we review the priorities specified in the "Goals 2000" document it is clear that this and other outside pressures are being brought to bear on education to teach to the intellect through course work that is linear-sequential and logical, such as math, science and technology, at the expense of that which would encourage creativity, is cyclical in nature and requires introspection and intuitive thought, such as is found in arts-related courses. The increasing movement away from any type of balance between the two types of learning is detrimental to all the students in American schools, regardless of how well they are currently functioning.   In essence, what this trend amounts to is an erosion of the time allotted for childhood with its innocence, simplicity and soulfulness, and a corresponding increase in the time identified as adulthood, with its lack of innocence and the resulting complexity. It's a consideration our schools have either not taken into account or have discarded as unimportant. Yet as the wholesale dismissal of this takes place, we are concerned with the children who "grow up too fast", who don't enjoy school, who create havoc and destruction for themselves and others; who, in all reality, have been denied their very real need to be children and develop their soul. Instead, we devalue their innocence, burden them with complexity and encourage them to adulthood before they are ready. It is little wonder that we are now reaping those awful consequences of what is being sown.

It is an interesting, terrifying trend. As American youth have been stripped of their childhood by a world that seems to place no value on it and also through the dismissal of developmentally appropriate learning and balance within the public schools, those outside voices have capitalized on the trend, reinforcing the notion that children and adolescents have the same capabilities, needs and drives as fully-grown adults. We are constantly made aware of young people both within and outside of the schools have moved out of what were once considered typical childhood behaviors and into adult ones. Twelve and thirteen year old girls give birth and become single parents. Sixteen-year old youths work 20 to 30 hours per week at a "part-time" job so that they can keep up with the things that their peers do or have and we wonder why they can't succeed in school. Gun legislation is introduced to attempt to curb the growing number of teenagers who believe that they should have a gun in school, either for their own protection or because its "the thing to do". Drug-free school zones are created which

31

increase the penalties for those who would bring narcotics into school. The language and disrespect heard while walking down the halls of a typical high school would make the most hardened person cringe. Talk of sexual escapades is common place, and other adult behaviors, whether alcohol or tobacco use, living on their own, or attaining credit, are all common-place occurrences. While some of these things are more detrimental than others to the over-all health and well-being of a child, all guarantee an erosion of childhood already too short and too devoid of soul.

Within the schools of America, these problems with and among young people are looked at with a genuine care and concern. Politicians, psychologists, business executives, parents and anyone else troubled by what is going on with children offer honest opinions and well-meant suggestions as to what will best enable our youth to succeed not only within the schools but also within the world that they are destined to enter. The schools, so driven by these outside forces, work diligently at incorporating suggestions and outright demands given them. The problem is, in the process of attempting to keep a variety of outside factions and voices happy, the schools have moved steadily away from what was once their mission: teaching students in a way that allowed them a developmentally appropriate balance that naturally provided for nurturing both their intellects and their souls.

For some children, this has had more profound effects than it has for others. It is patently ridiculous to believe that all of America's school children have been educated away from a connection with their souls. Yet this movement away from childhood and away from balance has had ill effects on all students, but for some, the effects are much more pronounced.

WHICH WILL BECOME OUR LOST SOULS?

I think it was when I first realized that children were destroying themselves that I knew that something needed to be said. You can't work as an assistant principal whose primary function is working with those children often identified as "at risk" and not see and feel the effects of what happens when children have lost touch with their souls. For me, as I work with young people who struggle in school both academically and socially, I am regularly struck by the similarities found in virtually all those who do not do well. Likewise, because I am regularly in contact with a variety of students who function either fairly well or exceptionally well, it is easy to see the differences between the two. Truly we learn through contrast and the contrast between the students who are surviving in our schools and the ones who are not is painfully apparent.

Before examining generalizations of the two types of students found at either end of the educational spectrum, I return you briefly to the concept of the soul: that it is an entity through which all our creative thoughts and ideas flow; through which we gain wisdom and insight into right and wrong; and through which we establish our emotional health and well-being and develop a strong and vital character. I return you as well to those things that the soul needs for full exercise and development: simplicity, self-reliance, creativity, beauty, freedom, love, faith and an appreciation of the cyclical process of nature. In remembering these you may be better equipped to see the contrast between the well-functioning student and the student who often either slips or gets pushed through the cracks of America's public schools.

Whenever I think of a soulful student, I can't help but think of Michael, a student I got to know very early on during my career as an administrator, while I was still directing drama productions, a left-over from my time teaching theater classes. Michael fit the profile of an average, well-functioning high school student. He had progressed through the school system as expected, successfully completing all classes and course work attempted. As I recall, disciplinary problems were minimal, his attendance was good and while he excelled in math and science, he was also heavily involved and met his need for creativity and fun through his work in the theater as well as on the school's basketball team. Teachers reported him to be a pure joy in the classroom, willing to help and to work hard, easy to get along with, well-liked. All in all, Michael was a teacher's ideal student.

If you explored Michael's background, you would find that the home he came from consisted of an intact, functional family with parents who had placed Michael and his two brothers at the center of their priorities and who had nurtured and guided them in positive ways, cultivating their strengths as opposed to their weaknesses. Since they were small, Michael and his brothers had been allowed natural ways to grow, to create and to develop a trust in themselves. I remember talking to his parents at his graduation party where I had commented to his mother that I could only hope that my own children turned out as healthy, balanced and complete as Michael had. As she spoke to me briefly about their desire to instill in their children solid core values, to allow them to make age-appropriate choices, to maintain their identity as a family unit and to give all her children opportunities to explore where their individual talents and strengths were, I couldn't help but smile at how much of what she said closely connected to the things that developed that most essential part of their being. To me, it was no wonder that Michael and his brothers were functioning so well as they moved through life. Their parents had assured them a connection to their souls.

Since so much of life follows a circular pattern, it was also no surprise to me that Michael had moved through the educational system so well. He fit the age-old expectation of what qualifies as a "good" student, and as he had moved through the system, he had been rewarded for fitting the expectation. His teachers, like his parents, guided and nurtured him in positive ways, due in large part perhaps to the fact that they found it rewarding to work with him and he made it easy for them. Michael naturally followed the expectations of the school and of the society at large. He had found ways to achieve in the regular classroom setting as well as ways to exercise his creativity and individuality that met societal and school definitions of what was acceptable and good. Because he had a balance, he was satisfied within the school setting and continued on the path he had chosen. Continued participation and success was cultivated and promoted by both the parents and adults within the schools and its continuation was ensured. Without question, all of this met Michael's needs to be accepted, loved and appreciated and he had moved forward through his education, remaining in school and contributing to it. For him, and for students like him, it is a self-perpetuating circle that serves them well, for not only are they meeting the definition of success, they are also doing so in ways that allow for exercise and nurturing of the soul.

Michael was by no means an exception to the rule as to what qualifies as a "good student". Invariably, the students that we find doing well and succeeding within the classrooms across America are those who are well-balanced. For these children, the circle they find themselves in is an efficient and beneficial one. Their success in the classroom setting enables them to avoid having to repeat any core classes and they are more likely to have the time to fit elective classes into their school day. Because of this, they are more likely to enjoy school and to connect with it, and often join in extra-curricular areas where the soul does have the opportunity to be exercised and stretched and to grow, such as the fine and performing arts. Through such areas students become involved in creating things of beauty. Through this creative process, they experience that sense of pride and fulfillment that causes the heart to swell. They work with others, thereby finding opportunity for the love and friendship that so touches the soul. In these areas, they also find themselves without any clear-cut, linear paths to follow and must reach inside the depths of their beings to come up with the methods and answers that will move them to the place where they want to be. There is no right or wrong to the process or the end result, only the satisfaction of recognizing that what they have done is wholly their own, with nothing like it before or since. They are allowed to operate with a measure of simplicity that requires no intricate technology or complex procedures and processes for success. Talk to any student following the completion of an artistic endeavor and you will find yourself speaking with a truly happy individual who sees value and worth in what has been accomplished.

That the students who are engaged in such opportunities are among the most successful in American schools has never surprised me much, though it has amazed some of my friends and colleagues who wonder how these students can do so well when they always seem to be among the busiest of the students within the schools. We know that curricular requirements are constantly being tightened up and more and more is demanded of students, yet those who engage in the extra-curricular areas, though their time is even tighter than those who do not, as a general rule attain at a higher level scholastically than those who are not so engaged. I say this doesn't surprise me for the simple reason that if a student has the outlets to provide for such exercise to the soul, they are happier. A student who is happy is much less likely to engage in non-productive creations or to wallow in a hardship mentality and display the problems that result. As less time is devoted to the negative things around them and more time is spent in creating and producing those things that bring joy and contentment, the student has more time to work in other areas as well, including the intellectual. Simply stated, the student has a balance between the intellect and the soul and the student achieves well within the schools.

For the students at the other end of the educational spectrum, the picture is a very different one. Where Michael was the stereotypical example of a "good" student, I vividly remember Stephen, a study in contrast from Michael, who was regularly referred to by other students and staff as a "bad kid" or a "trouble maker". I always felt that such terms when applied to Stephen, or to the numerous students like him, were misnomers for the simple reason that I never saw him or those like him as "bad kids", rather children who periodically did bad things. Likewise, I didn't see him or the others so much as trouble makers but rather students who had yet to learn the value in making positive contributions and creations. Be that as it may, Stephen, like other students who were disruptive to the educational process within the school, regularly made his way to my office when he had committed one of his many transgressions against the school or classroom rules.

Within the high school setting, Stephen struggled from the outset with the educational system. Having enrolled in no classes that he might find simply enjoyable, he was enrolled in the standard academic fare, none of which suited him particularly well. Perhaps because his day to day schedule was not need-satisfying, his attendance was poor and from the outset he was caught up in a vicious circle of missing instruction, failing assignments and tests, getting irritated, skipping more school, and so forth. When he did attend classes, he worked diligently at disrupting what was going on within the classroom, continually earning trips out of the classroom, to my office, to eventual suspension--simply more time out of the classroom.

This being the case, it is certainly little wonder that at the end of Stephen's freshman year, he had earned only one credit, having passed his two semesters of physical education, but nothing else. Not only had his freshman year been marked by failures, it had been also been marked by so many disciplinary problems, for everything from fighting to vandalism to drug use, that it was clear that Stephen was not a student likely to connect with or remain in the school setting. As he progressed through the system and throughout the years that I knew him, this fact of Stephen's life never changed. As is typical with the student who has no connection with the school, extra-curricular activities were never a part of Stephen's short-lived academic career, and he experienced no success and no satisfaction, either inside or outside of the classroom.

Sadly, for Stephen and so many students like him, the school served as only one more place in his world where dysfunction was the norm. Though I never had opportunity to speak with his parents at his graduation party, I did have numerous occasions to talk with them during the times when he was being suspended from school and I was seeking their assistance in helping Stephen find a path to success. Again, a study in contrast from Michael, Stephen's home life consisted of a mother and a step-father, the latter whom had no time to bother with this 15-year old problem that he had inherited through marriage. The mother, perhaps well-meaning and intentioned, had no idea how to set guidance and structure for her son, and though I had not yet met the younger child in the family, through our conversations I guessed that she was without limits as well. Both parents worked at a local factory, leaving for work at 6:00 a.m. and not returning home until after 4:00 p.m., and by their own admission, the two children were pretty much left to their own devices in terms of getting up, getting to school and getting home. Latch-key children since second grade, both children had come to depend on the television and video games for instruction and entertainment. Though she was aware of homework not completed and days of absence from school, the mother was reluctant to provide for any discipline or consequences that might address such problems. Nor was she or the step-father willing to modify their own life styles to create more structure for the children. Given their home situation, I often found myself generally impressed that Stephen and his sister managed to make it to school at all.

Where I had been able to smile during my conversation with Michael's mother and how her description of raising a functional child so closely connected with developing a soulful child, my conversations with Stephen's parents caused me grief, since they so vividly illustrated what happens when you leave the soul unattended and neglected. Given the absence of core values, no opportunity to develop trust in himself, no understanding or appreciation of creativity, no natural means to grow and develop his own talents and an education through the television that had been his babysitter for so many years, it was little wonder that he was not functioning well. When this was coupled with a total lack of family identity and an unformed sense of love and belonging, that Stephen was a soul-less child did not surprise me at all. The education he had received from his parents and the media since birth had precluded it.

With Stephen, I did what I so often did in looking for clues as to how best help a student, and that was to search through his cumulative file. The history it presented verified the vicious circle that Stephen was caught up in and showed that the problems had begun long before he enrolled in high school. It revealed a gradual decline in test scores and course grades and an increase in behavioral difficulties and absenteeism, beginning in the later elementary years. This decline in scores and grades and his mental withdrawal from the school setting was illustrated by what was perhaps the most poignant part of his file--the pictures. These offered a visual image of this child from kindergarten through high school. It was hard to look at those smiling faces from the early grades gradually be transformed into other sullen and angry ones as he had moved through the system, to the most recent picture. This last was absent even the anger in his eyes, rather a look that could only be called dull and lifeless--without soul.

As I looked through Stephen's file, it was quite easy to trace that somewhere around the sixth or seventh grade he had determined that school was not a place where his needs would be met and he had begun his rebellion. Records from teachers showed a general concern with the problems and disruptions he was creating, as well as a clear documentation of his academic difficulties. As this had occurred, his treatment within the school setting had undoubtedly deteriorated as well. Anger was generated on his part as he met continual dissatisfaction as well as on the part of the school staff who were more and more frustrated with his refusal to conform. And with this, his rate of failure and disciplinary problems had increased and any chance of him connecting positively with the school decreased. Stephen now found himself caught up in a situation where he had to repeat the basic core classes required and had even less opportunity for choosing to enroll in classes where he might find enjoyment and fun, or chances to exercise his own creativity and individuality. It was little wonder that as Stephen's frustration and dislike of school had continued to mount he had not availed himself of any of the extra-curricular offerings that could have offered positive avenues to the things that could have nurtured his soul. The relevance of Thomas Moore's words as to what happens when the soul is neglected was crystal clear with Stephen, for by the time I found myself working with him, he was displaying all those tendencies towards obsessions, addictions and violence and he showed through his actions that he suffered from a total loss of meaning so likely among those whose souls have not been nurtured.

By Stephen's junior year, his educational career was at an end. I wish I could say that as an organization, the school was able to provide appropriate intervention and break him out of the vicious circle he was so trapped in, but it just never happened. He continued to create havoc and disruptions as his junior year got underway, often preventing teachers from maintaining a positive classroom climate. An angry student, he continued to create a like anger among other students who failed to understand why he had to be "so different" and among his teachers who were, by that time, totally frustrated with his behavior and his refusal to conform. This anger led to even greater anger on Stephen's part and he escalated behavioral problems. Finally, having realized that a diploma was just not in his future, Stephen dropped out of school. Six months later, I read in the paper that he had been sentenced to a year in jail for breaking and entering and probation violations. It was clear that his future as one of society's lost souls had been assured.

The foregoing are both stereotypical examples of the students found at either end of the educational spectrum in American schools and it would be ridiculous to believe that there are not a large number of students of either type who do not fit into a similar picture. Likewise, there are a multitude of students who fall somewhere in between these two extremes, many of whom walk a fine line between success and failure. Regardless of the "type" of student, the bottom line is that all have a need to develop and strengthen the soul, yet there is less and less in the schools that allows this to happen. As schools are pressured by outside voices to provide students with an education that will render them well-skilled and able to be effective and efficient producers and consumers, and as this has been encouraged at earlier and earlier grades, there is much less time for students to engage in things that would nurture and exercise the soul. There is less time for introspection, less emphasis on the creative, less simplicity, less time for beauty, and less opportunity to develop self-reliance. For students like Michael, this movement has had less pronounced results. These students have blended into the educational setting thanks to a functional family and a solid connection with their soul from their earliest childhood. They will progress through the system as expected for the most part. School will be need-fulfilling, despite its emphasis on the linear and logical, and they will naturally pursue those things that will further the development of their soul through arts, athletics or other extra-curricular activities.

For students like Stephen, on the other hand, the movement away from soul-development has had and will continue to have more severe results. As the emphasis on the intellectual, logical and technical increases, the course work that has traditionally been difficult for them becomes more so. For many such children, their only exposure to soul-nurturing activities once came through school, and even in the best of situations, time for this is more and more rare. Worse, these children don't find themselves in the "best of situations", often repeating required classes that they struggle with. Coupled with the fact that they do not enjoy what they are being force-fed and that their days consist of nothing but such course work, their tendency towards failure increases and that vicious circle increases its strength and speed, leading many of these students to withdraw from the school setting.

These students are often easy to spot, practicing their need for individuality, creativity, even their own definition of beauty through their appearance and their demeanor. They feel a rebellion and a need to create and often do so by way of hair styles and colors, the clothes they wear and their pierced body parts. They elicit a certain shock among the adults in the society, most of whom view this as such children's primary intent. Few outside their own circle will view this as a form of creativity or art, and even fewer will see it as a means to exercise the creativity and individuality that their soul so craves. Rather, within the society and the educational system that houses them, they are viewed as different, disruptive and potentially dangerous. Because they are viewed as such, their treatment is different from that given to their more conforming counterparts and they become disconnected from the school setting. Nonetheless, though they are clearly not interested in the type of learning being offered, perhaps having no desire at this time in their lives to attend college, or go to work in some "boring" job, they are still provided with the same curricular requirements as their college-bound counterparts and those headed directly into the work force. The bottom line however tends to be that this only further alienates them from the school. Yet through the adults responsible for shaping their educational world, these students are continually force-fed those things that they see having little value or merit, under the well-intentioned guise that it will be "good for them in the long run". Educators need to step back and determine how few of these stick around for the "long run" and then objectively assess whether a "one size fits all" approach to education may be one of the causes for the high number of students that either disrupt the educational process or drop out of it entirely. There is some irony in the idea that the very thing that schools are doing to create efficient, productive workers for the society, is precisely what is pushing many of them out of education and into a world that finds them unskilled, unhappy and at odds with it. Rather than being effective and efficient, these are the "lost souls" like Stephen that are unable to function or create productively and positively in the schools or the society at large.

BUT WHY THE SCHOOLS?

For thirteen or so years of a child's life, he or she attends a typical American public school for six or seven hours a day, five days a week, 180 days a year. While this is statistically less time than will be spent in front of the television set, it is still a substantial amount of time that the child's body, mind and yes, soul, are left in the hands of those educators well-trained to teach. It is precisely for this reason that the schools are held responsible for the instruction of so many things beyond their one time charge of reading, writing and arithmetic. That teaching things once viewed as the domain of the home, such as sex education, conflict resolution, interpersonal communication, cultural diversity and basic life skills, has fallen to the schools is the sad consequence of a society where fewer and fewer families are devoting time to developing these in their children.

I had a conversation a while back with a colleague during which she made the comment that some children were already so destroyed by their home lives that there was nothing that the schools could effectively do to salvage their self-image, self-esteem and their happiness. I thought about that for a long time, questioning its validity in light of the fact that even the child from the worst possible home generally moved into the primary grades with a desire to learn, to create and to meet the expectations of their teachers. They seemed to have an inherent trust and a desire to love and be loved by those around them.

I remember well when this became clear to me. I'd had the opportunity to visit my daughter's kindergarten classroom as a "visiting story teller" during which I got to come in and spend a few minutes reading a story to all of the children in her class. As one of the city schools, the student body was a mixed collection of students of different races and socioeconomic backgrounds and her classroom was no exception. I remember how eagerly all of the students gathered as closely as they could, sitting cross-legged on the floor at my feet, wiggling closer and closer as I started to read. I looked up at the students periodically as I told the story, warmed by their rapt attention and sweet faces. One student, whose name tag read "Anthony", had wormed his way up to my chair, so close that had he moved any closer he'd have been in my lap. As I held up the book to show a picture, I looked at Anthony a bit closer. His clothes were mismatched, grubby and ill-fitting. His hair was tousled and dirty, and beneath untrimmed finger nails grime was embedded. Yet the look on his face as he looked at the picture was one of unabashed joy and anticipation.

I continued reading, realizing as I came to the last few pages that Anthony had moved and positioned himself so that he could rest his head against my leg as I completed the story. I

45

finished, reached down and ruffled his hair, only to be rewarded by one of the widest smiles I'd ever seen. I remember thinking wistfully to myself that such appreciation of simple things was tremendously rare among the teenagers that I worked with at the high school level.

I talked with the classroom teacher for a moment before I left, the students having readily moved back to their desks and their own reading books as she had instructed. I accepted her thanks for my willingness to read to the class, and thanked her in turn for allowing me the opportunity.

"I know it's none of my business," I told her. "But I'm interested in Anthony. He seems like such a sweetheart. Does he do okay in school? He looks as if his life might be a bit of a struggle outside of here."

"It's very sad," she sighed, lowering her voice so the students wouldn't hear. "His mother left him with his grandfather about a year ago. No one knows where she is. The grandfather's not exactly thrilled with raising a little boy, since he's very poor and not in the best health. There are weeks where Anthony wears the same clothes every day." She smiled sadly. "At this age, the children in his grade are still pretty oblivious to all that. But some of the bigger kids pick on him and tease him. I worry what's going to happen to him when he gets into the higher grades when the others make sport out of teasing kids like him."

I nodded and turned to leave, waving at my daughter who proudly waved her reading book at me as I made my way to the door. Just as I stepped outside, I noticed that Anthony was hiding behind the classroom door and he shyly stepped out and handed me a piece of paper. On it was written "Thenk yo" along with a drawing of a bright sun and a flower. He had apparently avoided his reading and created the picture while I was speaking with the teacher.

I knelt down and gave him a hug. "Thank you," I said. "You made my day."

It was hard not to think about Anthony after that and I've wondered what has become of him in the years since. As often happens with students in our city schools, he transferred elsewhere the following year, so my daughter was unable to let me know how he was doing. When I reflect back on that incident, I am still struck by the joy, love and trust that he was able to display, and this despite the fact that his life up until that point had not been one which would encourage the growth and development of such emotions. My fondest dream for Anthony was that he would be able to maintain that childlike innocence and connection with the soul and that somehow the schools would provide him with the exercise and nurture of that soulfulness that it seemed unlikely he'd get at home.

While I don't know what has happened to Anthony, it is not terribly hard to guess, since at the high school level, the teenage equivalents abound. After so many years as an assistant principal, it would seem that I would no longer be amazed by the fact that those students who struggle the hardest with school and with the system are almost without exception those students who had the soul sucked out of them at an early age, first through the home and then through the educational system. While they enter those early grades with that inherent trust, love and desire to learn, as they move through school the treatment they receive from peers and sometimes even adults is not the same as that received by those who, due to more functional home situations, are able to conform to specified standards, whether in appearance or behavior. With the difference in treatment comes first a disillusionment and then an anger and unhappiness with the school setting, and the problems begin. By the time they reach the high school level, the distrust and dislike of the school and those associated with it is well-ingrained in their consciousness and that vicious circle is fully established.

So I return to the question as to why the schools should shoulder the burden of nurturing and exercising the souls of their students. Beyond the fact that the public schools are the one place that we are assured that the vast majority of American children will attend, for more and more of our children, it is also the only place where many of our students, those from dysfunctional backgrounds and homes, will have the opportunity for the necessary development of the soul. Though many children may grow up in homes too often devoid of love, structure, and guidance, they are still in desperate need of these in order for them to become complete, fully functional adults. While in an ideal world, all homes would provide these for children, the reality is that it is just not occurring, and children that are entering schools across the country are displaying those symptoms that occur when the soul has been neglected. As this occurs, more and more of the time spent in the classrooms of our country is spent on managing and maintaining behavior problems and disruptions. Students act out, exhibiting disruptive, aggressive and even violent displays. Teachers and administrators find their time eaten up by classroom and school management problems with less time allowed for their primary mission--the education of students. Burn-out among educators is high as they lose their focus on why they entered the educational field. Students drop out or are kicked out of the school setting where they have failed to fit in and they enter the society totally unprepared for what life will bring them. And the society overall suffers as these students, still caught in the most vicious of circles, perpetuate the circle further, by parenting children as they've been parented and then sending these offspring into the schools to start the cycle again.

Without intervention, this circle continues and will continue into the foreseeable future. If you look again at the world around you, it is apparent how well established this cycle is. The preponderance of information concerning what is happening with American teenagers verifies this fact. A recent study conducted by the Carnegie Foundation reported that in 1992, children aged 12-15 were victims of assault more than any other age group and that in the twelve years between 1980 and 1992, the suicide rate among adolescents rose 120 percent. The study also pointed out that smoking by eighth-graders rose 30 percent from 1991 to 1994, that two thirds of eighth-graders had tried alcohol, and that the use of marijuana had more than doubled during that time. Equally frightening, the Foundation report cited that in 1988, 27 percent of girls and 33 percent of boys had experimented with sexual intercourse by their 15th birthday. In terms of school and their education, the report noted that only 28 percent of eighth-graders were proficient in reading.[4] This last should not come as a surprise to anyone. As children experiment with all of those things that arise from neglect of the soul, whether drugs and alcohol, sex or violence, there is less inclination to participate in those things that the school has to offer such as reading, and the schools are left dealing with the problems that these children are bringing with them into the school setting.

It often seems, however, that those of us within the schools would rather choose to ignore all the problems that are coming in as baggage with our students. The fact remains that we cannot ignore them because as long as those problems and difficulties are there, the students suffering from them are unable to learn, unable to connect with the school setting and unable to be fully functional and whether for the schools or for the society at large, the results of this are disastrous.

Schools are the one place where we can be assured that almost all children will attend at some point in their lives and it does seem to make sense that it is a place where it could be guaranteed that the soul would receive exercise and nurture. It makes sense as well that the schools themselves would directly benefit from an approach that did not neglect the soulful areas of education since these areas help students be more complete, happier and better balanced, regardless of the background they may come from. And the more whole our students are, the less likely they are to display all of those problems that so influence their own lives as well as the lives of those around them.

In the movie "Renaissance Man", the whole idea of nurturing and developing the soul in balance with the intellectual and societal needs is illustrated with poignant clarity. As the teacher, Danny DeVito is faced with the task of educating a small group of students so that they can pass a test and function efficiently in the military. Bringing with them varying degrees of dysfunction, the students illustrate clearly from the outset that they are not interested in the education, nor do they see themselves as capable, functioning humans, believing fully that they are indeed the "Double D's" (dumb as dog sh__) that the Army and others have labeled them.   While his task is to simply educate the students in language arts, Devito finds himself frustrated and at odds with the students and the dysfunctional behavior that they bring with them into the classroom in much the same way that a teacher does in any typical classroom.

When DeVito stumbles upon teaching them Shakespeare's *Hamlet*, it seems unlikely that the students will connect in any positive way and the military brass who have assigned him to the task of teaching see little merit in this group of students learning what they consider to be irrelevant lessons. Yet through creativity and alternative approaches to teaching and explaining the play, the students under DeVito's charge, do connect with the story and find creative, poetic and simple ways to understand the theme and beauty within, and through this, develop an inner trust and a self-reliance that had been absent before.

The movie is an exceptional illustration of what can happen when there is a balance provided between intellectual and soul development. While the students at the outset of the movie are clearly unhappy and at odds with the world around them, including the military, through the use of creativity, simplicity, beauty and poetry they develop into more whole beings, who then are able to move into the world that they are being prepared for, in this case, the military, with greater ease and comfort. In one particularly memorable scene, one of the students is challenged as to his knowledge of *Hamlet* by a superior officer who obviously places no value on such learning. With hesitation at first, but with growing pride and self-trust, the student recites from the play, as those who have been through the soul-developing lessons with him watch. The student himself seems almost rebuilt into a whole human, as do his counterparts through a vicarious sense of pride. Likewise, the superior officer develops a grudging respect towards this student and the others who show that they are now complete individuals. It is an important scene as it illustrates clearly that DeVito's students have achieved a balance between the needs of the soul and the need to be functional members of the military society they have entered.

There is no difference between the fictional characters in this movie and many of the students enrolled in schools across our country today. Many are viewed as the "Double D's" because their backgrounds and life experiences have not allowed them to be educated otherwise. They are viewed by the world around them as in desperate need of an education that will provide them with the knowledge and skills that will enable them to become proficient, productive members of the society that they will enter. The things that would nurture the soul are discounted as having value to these students in much the same way that *Hamlet* was viewed as without merit for DeVito's students. The outside voices of the world encourage the schools to burden these and all children with educational lessons in math, science, technology and workplace skills with a dismissal of opportunities within the schools to explore their inner most thoughts, their creative potential and their self-reliance.

At the end of the movie "Renaissance Man", the military invites DeVito back to teach a new group of students. Since they had viewed him and his lessons with Shakespeare with such distrust and misgivings at the outset of his work, their quiet acknowledgement of the value of what he had done is notable. It is almost as if the military, not well known for encouraging anything other than development of soldiers who will be efficient in their ranks, has accepted and perhaps even come to appreciate what can occur when the soul is developed in conjunction with the intellectual needs of an individual. It is a lesson that American public schools need to take into consideration as well. When we provide students, regardless of the background they come from or the problems that they bring with them, with activities and opportunities for soul development, we are that much more likely to provide them as well with the potential to develop into whole and happy individuals, who will not only operate more effectively and appropriately in the world around them, but also within the schools.

There is a final analogy that might be offered so as to explain why the exercise and nurture of the soul should fall within the province of the schools of America. I often conceptualize the soul as the most basic part of a human being, the necessary foundation of a person in much the same way as a concrete, solid base is a necessary part of a well-constructed house. If, through poor workmanship or other ineffective methods or behaviors, the foundation of this house is eroded or weakened, the house itself is less likely to remain solid, whole and functional, with the potential to collapse and cause harm to both those in and around. It only makes sense when one is working with such a house where the foundation has been poorly constructed, damaged or weakened, to provide it with reinforcements, corrections, and greater stability so as to assure its well-being and usefulness in the future.

The souls of our students are no different than the foundations of our houses. When they arrive in our schools poorly constructed, damaged or weakened, it is in our best interest as educators to provide them with those things that will reinforce, redevelop and rebuild this necessary base of their humanity. Since we can do this in such simple, cost-effective and efficient ways through the use of things already in place within the schools, there should not be a question as to how we can afford to do this, rather the question should center around how we can afford not to. By neglecting those things that allow our students to develop their strength, their self-reliance, their creativity and their sense of love and belonging and placing our whole focus on those things that will provide them with workplace knowledge and skills, we do nothing more than add a roof and some siding to structures that won't remain standing and functional long enough to make use of them.

PART II

Reconnecting Our Students to the Soul

Despite the fact that it has been mentioned more than once that the schools are the logical place where a reconnection to the soul could be provided to our children, I, as an educator, well recognize the outcries of disgust and the "Here we go again!" complaints that will follow any suggestion that the schools incorporate one more thing into their already burgeoning load. Yet the schools can provide exercise and nurture to the souls of all students, regardless of how they are functioning, without any major changes or expenses. It only requires a focus and appreciation of why doing so is important to the overall health and well-being of both the children in our charge, and also to the overall health and well-being of our society.

It is said that when a child is born into the world, he or she enters it "tabula rasa" or as a blank slate, ready to be written on by the experiences that life presents and whether directly or indirectly, these experiences are provided by the humans in a child's life. French philosopher Jean Jacques Rousseau noted, "Everything is good as it comes from the hand of the author of nature; but everything degenerates in the hand of man."[1] It can well be challenged that not everything is spoiled by man's influence, but it is difficult to dispute that our experiences and lessons are undeniably colored by that influence. For some of the children in American schools, the experiences and life lessons they have received have allowed them to maintain some degree of connection to their soul. For others, seemingly growing in numbers, their experiences and lessons have been ones that have severed their connection to soul and without intervention that provides for a reattachment, the ability for these to complete school and to move into society as functional members is greatly decreased, and in the meantime, their neglected souls make themselves known and affect not only themselves, but all those around them as well.

It is easy to understand the anger, denial and frustration felt by educators who often see themselves and the schools being scapegoated as the sole failure in developing successful adults for today's world and that is not the intent here. The educational system of this country should not be seen as the lone perpetrator of the problems in the society at large, particularly in light of the fact that their actions have been the result of pressures brought to bear by a variety of outside influences, including state and federal governments, special interest groups and business and industry, as well as the fact that they are faced with more and more children whose primary educators prior to school have been the media. Education's willingness to bow to the outside pressures and to modify curricular requirements at the expense of what is truly best for the children within their settings is that for which they should bear guilt. American schools with their free public education is the one thing that is guaranteed and available to every child within this country. In business terms, the children are the customers to be served by the schools, not the numerous outside influences. It is within the classrooms of these schools that those things that are truly the most necessary to becoming a successful, functioning, happy and whole adult have the potential to be nurtured and developed. Yet as the schools bow to outside pressures in order to meet the demands of business and industry, politicians and others who have no clue as to the developmental needs of a child or a child's soul, they do a tremendous disservice to their true customers by curtailing and limiting areas of creative expression, introspection and the things that are intuitive and develop a sense of self-reliance, freedom and love.

So before educators and others continue the push towards increasing requirements and demands in the areas that are intellectual, logical and linear-sequential, perhaps it will better serve all concerned to consider how easily a balance can be provided between these and those areas that nurture the soul. In doing so, they may also come to see that providing for such balance simply makes good sense in terms of the future for our children and ourselves.

CHAPTER 3

The Need for Self-Reliance

From the time a child exits the womb, every action and movement that is attempted brings him one step closer to that independence and self-reliance that all humans crave. In the initial months and years of a child's life, he is wholly dependent upon the adults who are responsible for him, and as he progresses through late childhood and early adolescence, his need for independence and his ability to take care of himself increases. Often, the adults in his life are either frustrated or scared by this process, yet it is a natural, normal need that in few, if any, cases can be circumvented. How the child develops the independence is the question that needs to be answered here if one is to fully understand how important this self-reliance is to the exercise and development of the soul.

So as to offer definition to the whole concept of self-reliance, it should probably first be noted that self-reliance is not simply the physical ability to care for yourself and your needs, but is as well the whole ability to listen to and heed that inner voice; to have a high degree of self-trust. While the ability to care for one's physical needs has great value and validity, it is not nearly as vital to a person's emotional health and wellness as is the ability to heed that wisdom that arises from the soul and provides emotional strength and stability. It is through this self-reliance and the ability to tune into the wisdom of the soul that provides a person with his ethics, his values and his principles. Without such ability a person is that much easier swayed towards the messages, constantly changing and mutable, being sent from those loud and powerful outside voices. He becomes that rudderless ship mentioned earlier that moves with whatever current is the strongest. What's worse, all too often, what is being sent and sold via these has little or no value, changes from day to day with the tenor of the times, and can serve to make the receiver and buyer of those messages wholly non-self-reliant.

TODAY'S BRAVE NEW WORLD

A classic literary example of this and what happens to the soul when a person is conditioned by the outside voices of society is illustrated in Aldous Huxley's 1932 novel *Brave New World*. By using a technique called hypnopaedia, the residents of this society are indoctrinated through a form of sleep teaching, "...Till at last the child's mind is these suggestions, and the sum of the suggestions is the child's mind. And not the child's mind only. The adult's mind too--all his life long. The mind that judges and desires and decides--made up of these suggestions. But all these suggestions are our suggestions."[1] Though the novel might be considered a satire, it none the less said a great deal about the potential for control of the masses within society if they were conditioned by outside voices well enough to totally drown out the inner voices and the wisdom of the soul. Throughout the novel, the parallels found between the Brave New World that Huxley created and the movement of the world and society today strike many as frighteningly significant.

In Huxley's work, the masses are conditioned through this sleep teaching in much the same way as we are educated through television and the media, in both situations, society's members grow up believing that material goods and being effective producers and consumers is what is important in life. Whether in the fictional Brave New World or in our world today, there is an emphasis on participating in groups of all types, with time to spend alone either difficult to find or discouraged. The inhabitants of the Brave New World call their drug of choice "soma", while today we have those such as Prozac, both designed and consumed so as to disguise or dismiss the emotions that are experienced any time the soul is neglected. Other parallels are found as well, whether in the sexual promiscuity of the Brave New World and ours, in the technological advances found there and in our society, or in the tendency to want and gain instant gratification in those things we desire. In both worlds, that these things have become the norm is the result of the power of those outside voices in selling that what they are saying is correct and in both worlds, the ability to tune out these voices and not be overwhelmingly influenced by them is a nearly impossible task.

To take this concept a step further, consider the hypothetical question as to whether you could take a person, erase all the conditioning that he had undergone since birth and place him into our world, totally in touch with the soul and able to soulfully evaluate what was good and bad, right and wrong within the world around him. For those familiar with Huxley's work, they will recognize a similar case with the character of John, the "savage" who has not received the conditioning as have the residents of the Brave New World, and who, when brought into that society, finds himself at odds with it, a lone soulful character in a world devoid of soul. The person who is so at odds with the world fights a constant swim upstream. It takes a high degree of inner strength and conviction to fight the currents of the society and the times and remain in touch with the soul, holding firm to the wisdom and knowledge that is found there. For John, his fight to swim upstream, to not feel alienated in a world he is so counter to, and to maintain his connection with soul is a battle lost, and he surrenders the fight with self-mutilation and suicide, preferring that to becoming what those around him have become. For many people in our present world who find themselves at odds with societal norms and trends, it is possible that the outcome may be similar; perhaps not actual suicide, but an equally lethal emotional one. For any one, it is difficult at best to be out of the mainstream, but it is harder still when you are caught in a constant swim upstream against some incredibly strong currents that regularly push you away from that inner wisdom of the soul. When one surrenders to those currents--those voices--the ability to be self-reliant is eroded and there is a weakening which fosters even greater dependence and this dependence in turn leads to anger. And arising out of this anger is the "violence, addictions, and loss of meaning" identified by Moore as the sad result of a neglected soul.

It is one thing to look at self-reliance in a theoretical context but the whole concept is better served by now turning to those whom this book seeks to address--our young people as students in American schools. There is much that makes it clear that they have been moved further and further from self-reliance, and it is equally clear that there are ways that we can return to fostering self-reliance and its inherent soul-strengthening properties within those schools.

DEPENDENCY AND
THE LOSS OF SELF-RELIANCE

Very few students in the school could hold a candle to Suzanne in looks, appearance, grooming and outward behavior. A simply lovely child of 14 when she entered as a freshman, she had an engaging smile, a head of thick blonde hair, bright blue eyes and a sprinkling of freckles across her nose. To say she dressed well would be an understatement--she daily looked like she had stepped out of the pages of a teen fashion magazine. Coupled with the outward trappings, she had all the behaviors of a well-behaved, cooperative teenager. She was polite, courteous, respectful and helpful. Those of us who saw her in the halls or in the classroom naturally assumed that this was a freshman who would not only move happily through school, she would most likely find happiness beyond it as well.

We couldn't have been more wrong.

My dealings with Suzanne began toward the end of her freshman year when one of her friends approached me and asked what seemed to me an odd request. She wanted me to speak with Suzanne, because, as she put it bluntly, "She's going crazy and something's wrong. She's acting really weird and won't even talk to me anymore." Unfortunately, that didn't leave me with a whole lot of information to go on, and my inclination was to disregard the request and to pass it off as the outgrowth of some teenage disagreement. Yet when I saw Suzanne in the hall later that same day, she didn't seem her usual perky self. Her eyes seemed puffy and dark; her make-up not as carefully applied as usual and her clothing, black jeans and a black t-shirt, were a distinct departure from her usual wardrobe. I sent a slip for her to come to my office a short time later.

As she sat down in the chair next to my desk, a closer look

verified what I had observed in the hall. Suzanne looked awful. The puffy, dark circles under her eyes were more pronounced up close, and were topped by those blue eyes, now bloodshot and tired. Her hair, usually clean and well-styled, had been hastily tied into a pony-tail, as if she hadn't had time to wash or even comb it. And perhaps worse, her usual energetic manner of walking and carrying herself seemed to have vanished and she slumped in the chair, refusing to look at me.

I found myself tongue-tied, doubtful as to what to say to this teenager who seemed so different from the one who was usually in our halls. "I'm not quite sure how to begin this, Suzanne," I started. "It's none of my business; you're not in any trouble with your teachers or anything. Yet you just don't look like yourself, and I was concerned. Is there anything going on that I can help with?"

She continued to stare at the floor, saying nothing. But slowly a huge tear slipped down her cheek, rolling off her chin and onto her shirt. She ignored it as if pretending it wasn't there would keep me from noticing. I reached behind me and grabbed a box of tissue to place within her reach, and within seconds that first large tear was joined by others and soon her tiny frame shook with sobs.

"I can't tell you," she finally uttered, after the initial wave of grief had eased. "You'll tell my mom and she'll kill me." The sobs intensified again.

I allowed her some time to cry and allowed myself the time to choose my words carefully. "Suzanne, I want to keep your trust, but I won't lie to you and tell you I won't tell your mom about whatever this is, because if you're in some kind of trouble or danger, I have to tell her. But obviously something's really wrong, and if you don't want to talk with me, let me hook you up with someone you can talk to." She shook her head negatively, and I tried another tact. "Is this something that you're going to be able to solve on your own?"

She wiped tears off her face with a clenched fist and looked at me for the first time. "I've tried," she said. "And its only getting worse." I still don't know why she decided to open up at that point, but all of a sudden she began to talk, confessing that she had taken up what is commonly called "binging and purging". Suzanne was bulemic.

The story she told me, I now know, was not an uncommon one. Suzanne was in many ways a typical adolescent female who looked at herself in the mirror and viewed herself as fat, though nothing could be further from the truth. She told me how she had become obsessed with getting on the scale in the morning and before she went to bed and how even the slightest of weight gains caused her overwhelming panic. She had tried fad diets and exercised to the extreme, yet couldn't get past the idea that she was fat and if the scale showed an increase of a pound or two, she would starve herself until they had disappeared.

"But I like to eat," she said, almost apologetically. "And I read this article in a magazine about this girl who would eat anything she wanted, and then she'd go into the bathroom, make herself throw up, and it helped her keep her weight down. I know that story was saying that it was a bad thing to do, but all I thought was, 'Hey, I could do that'." The sobs started again. "So I tried it and it seemed to work, but its like, now, I can't eat anything at all without having to throw up. It's so gross and I'm so embarrassed and I'm scared to death."

My heart went out to this child, sitting in my office and so obviously in pain and fear and I knew that a problem of this magnitude was way beyond my capacity to help or to solve and that there had to be a parent involved. Yet I was fearful of betraying Suzanne's trust in anyway.

"I need you to listen to me for a second, Suzanne." I began slowly. "I don't want you to be mad or upset that you've told me all this, but its a problem that I don't have the skills to help you with effectively. In truth, there may not be much the school can do except suggest some places where you could get help, but to do that, we're going to need to talk with your mom."

"She'll kill me," she said dully. "Oh, she'd be nice in here with you, but once we got home, she'd let me have it. I can just hear it now. 'What are you thinking, Suzanne?'" she mimicked. "'What will people think? And to tell people at school about this! What were you thinking?'" She continued with a hollow laugh. "She'd be the picture of a good, concerned mom with you. But I'd never hear the end of it. No. You can't tell her, please."

"Then you're going to have to," I told her. "And I'll help you with that. But that is truly the only way that you have any chance of getting past this. It's not a problem I can teach you to resolve, and you've already said it's not one you've been able to resolve on your own." We spent the next hour or so talking about the problems involved with talking to her mother. Whether real or imagined, Suzanne had a true fear that in admitting the bulimia to her mother, she would face other, equally unpleasant problems at home when the truth was out, particularly, it seemed, once her mother was aware of the fact that other people knew about it.

Since that fear was so real to her, I offered her a way out. "Talk to your mom tonight, Suzanne," I told her. "Take some time and sit down with her and talk to her about it in the same way that you did with me. You don't have to let her know that I know. Just that you're frightened and scared and think you need some help." Suzanne nodded slowly. "But let me know tomorrow how it went. Can you do that?"

Nodding again, she stood up and started for the office door. "I'll try to tell her," she said. "But she's gonna hate me."

The next morning, before classes had begun, I was startled from the paperwork in front of me by a knock on my office door. I looked up to see Suzanne there, her eyes full of tears, looking even worse than she had the day before. "Can I come in?" she asked.

I motioned her in and stood up to close the door. As I turned back to her, the tears began in full force. "It didn't go well?" I asked softly. "Tell me what happened."

"Worse than that," Suzanne said. "I couldn't tell her. She took one look at me yesterday when I got home and started yelling at me for 'going to school looking like that'. We got into a fight about how she spends all of this money so that I can have nice clothes and nice things and I go off to school dressed like that yesterday." The sobs started again. "She told me she was embarrassed and ashamed and that everyone would think she was a horrible mother. I couldn't tell her. She was just so mad, I didn't want to make it worse."

I sat quietly, letting the grief run its course. When the sorrow had subsided somewhat, I leaned forward. "Do you want to get past this, Suzanne?" I asked. She nodded. "Then I'll call her and we'll ask her to come in here."

"You're going to tell her?" she asked sadly. "I don't want you to do that."

"And you asked me not to, so I won't," I responded. "But I'll be here while you tell her and then we'll work through whatever comes so that you can get the help that you need and deserve." Suzanne looked doubtful. "Can you see another way?" I asked her.

"No," she admitted. "I can't tell her by myself."

"Then we'll do it together, but you'll do the talking and I'll be here for moral support."

I called Suzanne's mother at work right away, being put through to her office by a pleasant-sounding secretary who had informed her who was calling.

"What's this about?" she asked quickly. "Is there some type of trouble that Suzanne is in?" She laughed then, which seemed incongruous given the fact that Suzanne was, indeed, in some trouble that was certainly not laughable. Yet she sounded as if the call must be pertaining to some trivial, insignificant matter. Surely her daughter couldn't have a problem that a school official would need to call about.

"As a matter of fact, yes, there is some trouble--a problem that we need to talk to you about and I'd rather not go into it over the phone," I said. "Can you come into the school right away."

She seemed to sober a bit with that and assured me that she would be right in. While we waited, Suzanne and I discussed the difficulty of telling her mother about the bulemia. It was hard for me to believe that Suzanne was correct in her assessment that her mother would be angry with her for having a problem such as this, or for needing help. "It's not so much that," Suzanne told me. "It's that other people know about it. That's what's gonna make her mad."

Twenty minutes later, the secretary paged me to announce that Suzanne's mother had arrived. I looked at her and smiled. "Are you ready to do this?" I asked.

No. Suzanne said bluntly. "But I guess I have to."

When Suzanne's mother walked in the door, I was immediately struck by the fact that I was faced with another, slightly older version of the daughter, and this version appeared to be doing a fairly successful job of making sure she didn't look too much older. The hair was the same long, blond mane. The eyes the same bright blue, but expertly made up with shadow and mascara. She was dressed impeccably and expensively and carried herself with an air of confidence that could have easily been mistaken for arrogance. She refused the seat I offered her, and remained standing. "What's this all about." she asked. She seemed irritated--annoyed--and I was put off by the tone in her voice.

"Suzanne needs to talk with you," I began. "She's got a problem that she needs some help with and I told her I'd be here to offer her some support and to answer any questions that you may have once she's done." I looked at the girl, visibly trembling in the chair beside my desk. "It'd be easier if you'd sit down so that she can talk with you," I said.

The mother sat down then and for the next minutes, we waited in silence as Suzanne summoned up the courage to talk with her mother. Finally, after a number of false starts, the story began, re-told in much the same way as she had told me the previous day. When she finished, I looked at Suzanne closely. She had withdrawn visibly, shrinking into a little ball as she had finished, seemingly terrified of looking at her mother for the reaction. And as I turned to look at the mother, I understood the fear. On her face was an undisguised look of disgust and anger. This was replaced quickly as soon as she caught me looking at her, but she hadn't changed it quickly enough. Her attitude was plain and the new mask that she donned couldn't disguise it.

"Oh, dear." she said, with what seemed, and probably was, feigned concern. "I should have known something was wrong, sweetie. You just haven't been yourself lately, have you?" She looked at me. "My job just keeps me so busy, always running and traveling somewhere. They just can't do without me at work, and I'm afraid that I must have neglected seeing that something was up with her." She looked at Suzanne who still sat slumped in her chair. "We'll work this out right away, won't we, sweetie?" Suzanne still didn't look at her, so she returned her comments to me. "I do appreciate your concern," she said. "I'll take care of this at home. My goodness!" she laughed then. "The things that they ask you school people to do these days! I don't know how you keep up with it."

Her dialogue was making me uncomfortable. I had difficulty understanding how this parent could apparently pass off such a serious problem as bulemia with such an obvious lack of sincerity or concern. "We do have a student assistance program," I offered, "So that if Suzanne needs some counseling or referral to a support group for teenagers with eating disorders, we could explore the possibilities with you."

I believe what was displayed in the mother's eyes then was pure anger, but she disguised it well. "Oh, no," she said. "We can take care of this ourselves, can't we, Suzanne? I've got wonderful insurance and all those benefits through my work, so if there ends up to be something she needs, we'll take care of it ourselves. We wouldnt want to bother the school with this little problem." She leaned over and kissed Suzanne lightly on the cheek. "We'll talk about this at home some more, sweetie. You have a good day at school now." With that, she swept out of the office, leaving the door open and waving cordially to the secretaries in the outer office.

I was chilled. Here was a mother who had just been informed that her daughter had a serious eating disorder, and she had passed it off as if it were the simplest of matters. Suzanne looked resigned and depressed. "That's my mom. Make sure everything looks good to everyone else." It appeared a very accurate insight.

———

I could write at great length about what transpired after this incident, about the continuing battles faced by Suzanne in attempting to get past the bulimia that had come to rule her life. We had numerous talks in the months and years that followed and while she did finally succeed in getting some professional counseling, her mother would regularly switch her from one therapist to another, almost as if she didn't want her daughter spending too much time with any one in particular. But Suzanne had developed a certain degree of strength and had joined a support group for teenagers with eating disorders that we had located. She unfortunately didn't have the strength to tell her mother that she was attending these sessions however, preferring to let her think that she was meeting with a weekly study group, rather than face her mother's certain disapproval. It is almost tempting to analyze the mother's behavior here, but such is not my purpose nor is it within the scope of my skills. At the end of her junior year, Suzanne was still battling the bulimia. She moved away just prior to her senior year, deciding to live with her father in Florida. I can only hope that he has been more supportive and helpful with her problems. I may never know.

While I say it is not within my ability or skill to analyze either Suzanne or her mother, there are some points to be drawn from their story that relate to that whole idea of self-reliance. In looking at Suzanne and her battle with bulimia, it was clear that though she was neither fat nor even slightly overweight, the inner voice that could have told her this was virtually inaudible. She was not unlike thousands and thousands of other girls who have been raised in a world where the media and others promote the idea of beauty and health as one inseparable from thinness and who will do anything to attain that supposed ideal. Countless articles and studies point to this fact. You can return to the idea that over time, millions of teenagers, both girls and boys have been taught the "two plus two equals three" lesson. Many of them have bought into it with all they have, wholly disregarding the wisdom of their inner voice and their soul that would tell them that it is an inaccurate lesson. So whether it be eating disorders such as anorexia and bulimia in an effort to be thin, or steroid use in an effort to "bulk up" the muscles of the body, countless numbers of teenagers continue believing an inaccurate lesson and displaying the problems that result.

"Problems occur when a person behaves accurately on inaccurate information," someone once told me. This is the case here and with many of the other problems that teenagers today are finding themselves involved in. The information that they have been fed over time is just that--inaccurate. And if it is not inaccurate, their life experiences and lessons have not allowed for them to assess it in the correct way. Messages that promote health and wellness are not inappropriate or damaging to the person who understands that eating right and exercising are valuable in maintaining physical health. But if the information is interpreted inaccurately or if someone is obsessed with their appearance and believes that the only way to be seen as beautiful and healthy is through model-like thinness or body-builder type muscles, and if they perceive they don't measure up to the standards despite all attempts, they are more likely to be swayed to extreme measures to get there.

Suzanne was a classic example of someone who had never learned to assess information for its accuracy nor to heed her inner voice for assistance. Since she'd been small, her life lessons had been ones that centered around the idea that what other people thought was of utmost importance. Her mother's attitude had made that crystal clear. She had made sure that her daughter always dressed impeccably, was well-groomed and displayed an outward appearance of normality. Her phrase

"What will people think?" was the regular question that she had issued any time Suzanne had done something that she believed was less than perfect. It was, however, virtually impossible for Suzanne to maintain such standards and in an effort to do so, she had succumbed to what seemed the only possibility--bulemia.

"Nature suffers nothing to remain in her kingdoms which cannot help itself," wrote Emerson. "The genesis and maturation of a planet, its poise and orbit, the bended tree recovering itself from the strong wind, the vital resources of every animal and vegetable are demonstrations of a self-sufficing and therefore self-relying soul."[2] It is unfortunate that so many people, both young and old, have been encouraged away from self-reliance, since the inevitable result is a weakening such like that seen with Suzanne. If the lessons to rely on what others think is pervasive and persuasive enough, over time any one can lose the ability to think for themselves or trust the voice of their soul. Once this has occurred, reliance on the outside voices and what they say and sell is invariably the result and this reliance causes a lessening in the ability to be self-reliant in the future and sets up a vicious circle. As the person finds himself wholly reliant on things outside of himself for his health, happiness, security, peace of mind, or anything else, he has given up his ability to take care of himself. He has accepted the crutch provided by the outside forces and becomes wholly dependent on it. This dependency is a violation of a human's nature, and through its continuation the soul is further weakened and diminished. Yet nothing in what such a person has been taught or learned has developed self-sufficiency or self-reliance and so, thus weakened, he continues on with growing dissatisfaction and unhappiness to find something outside himself to believe in or to provide instant happiness, gratification and strength. Sadly, there will most likely be an outside voice that will crop up with an offer to provide just that, but for a price that, when paid, will remove the person more and more from the simple satisfaction the world around could offer and the simple truths that could be heard through the voice of the soul.

When the soul is nurtured and exercised through self-reliance, it promotes self-reliance in return. It is little wonder then that those people without the connection to the soul and the self-reliance it can provide suffer so much discontent. The circle that they find themselves in, perhaps initially not of their own creation but created by the powerful influences in their lives, is one that they feel powerless to break, if they even realize that they are trapped in one at all. From their reliance on things outside of themselves, they find themselves slaves to any number of things, whether eating disorders such as Suzanne's, or drugs, alcohol, sex, or whatever it may be that they think will bring them happiness. For those of us who teach and work within the schools, we are stunned by the numbers of students who come to us each day displaying such disorders and the problems that result. As we recognize this as a natural outgrowth of the world they are being educated by, it becomes obvious that the schools need to provide some avenue for students to begin to either develop or strengthen their means of becoming self-reliant souls.

SELF-RELIANCE IN SCHOOLS

It isn't a question of whether schools and those who are involved in them should provide avenues to develop their students' self-reliance, it is a necessity. Suzanne's problems were mainly detrimental to herself, yet numerous other students who have no ability to trust themselves or the wisdom of their souls come into schools daily displaying all types of problems that result from reliance on the outside voices of this world. Some display the problems associated with their learning over time which has convinced them there is no need to treat others with respect; others may succumb to the peer pressure so prevalent and involve themselves with drugs, sex or violence. Whatever inaccurate information and learning that they are bringing with them has ill effects not only on them, but on those around them as well.

I mentioned earlier in discussing why the schools should foster soul that to do so didn't necessarily call for any curricular changes nor did it call for any extra expenditures of time or money. It simply calls for a modification in the way we are doing things and a return to the balance in what we choose to teach. Certainly this is true in the nurturing of soul through self-reliance. I have been both amused and saddened by some of the recent educational trends that have spoken to a movement away from teaching students anything that might call for rote memorization, whether as basic as learning their multiplication tables or as complicated as learning all the amendments to the Constitution. The theory has been, it seems, that it is more important for students to learn where and how to access the information as opposed to having it at their ready disposal through the memorization process. This trend however, promotes a reliance on things outside the student for the information that they may require. As always, there is validity in this in part, for the ability to know how and where to access information is tremendously important in the world we live in.

But process through both the short term benefits and the long term results, and you'll realize that the bottom line is the creation of a student who must depend on the availability and the accessibility of those resources and, God forbid, those become unavailable or inaccessible, there is some question as to whether the student will be able to successfully function in completing an assigned task or project. If not, it is fairly certain that anger and frustration will be the result. Ask any educator what happens when a student becomes angry and frustrated and you will hear stories of classroom disruptions, failed assignments, missed school days, and a variety of other problems.

It is not just in the need to go outside oneself to access general information that is the resultant problem. Perhaps more important is what this education takes from students in terms of their ability to be self-reliant. Through such a method, students are inescapably educated that they are not capable of relying on their own minds or memories for information--that they must seek outside themselves for what it is that they need. This is a powerful lesson that translates into other areas as well. If they are so dependent upon outside sources for basic information, it is only logical that they would seek outside themselves for answers to life's more difficult questions as well. Should I skip school today? Should I sleep with my boyfriend? Is it okay to do this drug, just this once? How can I be more popular? Whatever the question is, if it is answered through the outside voices, whether the media or the peer group who has been unavoidably educated by it, the answer is often much different than the one that arises from the wisdom of the soul.

I remember how clear this became to me one day when I was working in my office with a student by the name of Jack, a regular visitor to my office. I enjoyed my visits with this child immensely, despite the fact they invariably arose from a time when he had committed yet another transgression and was facing the penalty for it. Invariably during these meetings, I found myself immersed in an in-depth conversation with a young man who had an incredible mind and who easily met me at my level and at times surpassed me. As we talked one day, I became aware of a pattern in his communication that I had not previously paid any attention to and that was his use of the term "but" which followed any statement that he made about what he should have done or should be doing.

The situation this day centered around Jack's decision to draw some rather creative graffiti on his desk which the teacher determined merited a detention during which he could wash all the desks in the classroom, which Jack in turn determined merited a very audible "Bull shit!" which greatly amused the rest of the students. When the teacher in her frustration ordered him out of the room and to the office, he determined that, being it was a nice day outside, he may as well just skip the remainder of school and go enjoy himself somewhere off school property.

When he returned the next day, he found himself summoned to my office to explain the happenings of the previous day and to face the consequences. I began our discussion in an effort to get him to identify where he had erred and how the situation could have been avoided.

"Hi, Mrs. L.," he smiled in his characteristic way as he entered my office. "Is there a problem?"

I had to grin at that. He knew full well what the problem was but believed if he was charming and clever enough he just might talk his way out of it. "Why don't you tell me, Jack," I countered. "How did English go yesterday?"

"Oh, that," he said. "It's not a big deal. Mrs. Jones and I just had a little misunderstanding. I'll be sure to apologize in class today. If that's all, I'd better be..." He moved towards the door.

Hold on a minute, Jack," I said. "The apology is appropriate, but there's more here that we need to talk about. Why don't you tell me what you were thinking?"

"I was just bored," he sighed. "I hate that stupid story we're reading, it has no meaning whatsoever and I just got to doodling. I knew I should pay attention, especially since there's a test on it next week and I really need to pass, but I knew I probably won't, so I just got distracted."

I knew the story being read and could in many ways understand Jack's inability to focus. Regardless, it was one of the hoops he needed to jump through in order to move through the class in the prescribed way and it served no purpose to dismiss at least that much of its importance. "I'll agree that the story isn't all that great and I'll also agree you probably do need to pass the test. In which way were your chances for that better? By making at least an attempt to pay attention or by giving up and doodling on the desk?"

"Tough question, Mrs. L.," he said with a little grin. "I think you know the answer to that but I'll play along. I should have sucked it up and paid attention despite the fact that the story is bull, is useless and has absolutely no relevance to anything." This in a mock serious tone, but the manner in which he continued was fully serious. "I want to pass that class, Mrs. Lawrence. I really do. God forbid I have to repeat all that junk. And I know that I need to work harder and pay attention, but it seems pointless. Mrs. Jones tells me all the time I probably can't pass this semester. She once asked me why I even show up in class, since I'm bound to fail."

Our conversation continued in much the same vein, with repeated statements by Jack of what he knew he should and should not have done in the situation, whether in using inappropriate language, or in leaving the school grounds. As the statements went on I became more and more focused on the fact that following each and every accurate statement of what he should have done was the term "but" and a very rational sounding explanation of why he had not done it.

"Tell me something, Jack," I said. "Can you tell me a time when you've known what you should do, but instead listened to that part of you that offered an excuse for not doing it? And can you give me one example of a time when doing exactly that didn't get you into some kind of trouble?"

As we played through a variety of scenarios, both Jack and I realized that, unequivocally, each time he was faced with a situation in which he knew what he should do yet responded to the "but", he was always finding himself in actual or potential trouble. To the contrary, on those occasions when he actually listened to the first instinct he had, he did the right thing and no trouble followed. For both of us, the meeting had profound implications. He started to focus more on what his first inclination for behavior was and made slow but steady progress in staying out of trouble. I knew with certainty that what Jack was learning to listen to was the inner voice of his soul and that he was developing self-reliance and self-trust as a result, and the consequences meant much less trouble for him in school.

We can look at students like Suzanne and like Jack and realize that in one way or another, there are tremendous outside influences and pressures being brought to bear on them. As more and more students are raised in homes where there has been no instruction on how to develop self-trust and self-reliance in sorting through such outside voices, they are more likely to accept what is purported as truth. When this occurs, the times when they hear the inner voice telling them what is truly correct, it is likely dismissed with a "but" followed by some plausible excuse created by the education of those outside voices. They will then find themselves in some type of trouble, either real or potential.

After that day with Jack, I carefully observed and recorded

how often a child would come into my office and tell me with absolute accuracy what they should have done while in the same breath offer a rational sounding excuse, always prefaced with "but", for why they did otherwise. I witnessed this with everything from the simple behaviors such as skipping ("I knew I shouldn't go to the beach, but all my friends were going.") to the most extreme offenses including bringing a weapon on to school grounds ("I thought it was a bad idea, but I thought so and so might be after me.") The more this pattern repeated itself, the more certain I became and I started working diligently with these children to help them see that trusting that first instinct, that inner voice of their soul, could help keep them out of trouble and place them on another, more successful, path.

While I have always believed that my job was to help students find pathways for success, I should clarify here that as this awareness dawned, I was not either brave or stupid enough, depending on your point of view, to use the term "soul." Since the soul is, as noted, viewed as a religious concept, to bring it up within the walls of an educational institution is to court trouble. Rather, I was likely to use the analogy of the stereotypical cartoon image of a character with a tiny angel perched on one shoulder and a little devil on the other, each preaching their individual agenda. I could identify this to the students as the angel representing their conscience, an acceptable term, and the devil as being the voice that would encourage them to disregard what they knew to be right. The students could well understand this concept and it caused no discomfort for anyone since there was no reference to the soul. I will add here that I was wise enough not to use the same analogy with my colleagues since it was much too simplistic for their logical and rational minds, and the term "soul" would be one that they'd likely dismiss outright. So I suffered the discomfort of keeping silent about something that I believed strongly to be true in order to meet the comfort levels of those around me. I was aware that to do otherwise and force-feed anyone the concepts had the potential to cause anger, fear or both and would not be productive. This whole idea and the problems associated with trying to change or sway large group thoughts and processes such as those associated with educational decision making is an area deserving further exploration and is one which will be developed more in Chapter Nine, The Making of Educational Decisions.

The schools have a need, not only in the best interests of the children they serve but also for their own well-being and survival, to encourage self-reliance among their students. The child who has no self-trust, no ability to listen to the wisdom of the soul, is a child who, as noted, is weakened and dependent and who far too often ends up angry, and there are too many simple ways to provide for the development of this soul-need to simply disregard them. That the recent movement in the educational community has been away from such things that would nurture the soul has been discussed and it seems appropriate now to encourage a movement back towards some semblance of balance.

Perhaps the first things that schools need to provide for all students to this end is the opportunities to work in curricular areas where there is not a right and wrong pattern for the effective completion of a task. In math, science and technology, there is generally a specified means of proceeding through a given process. There is a place to begin and a clear end result; a linear-logical pattern of operation. In other areas the work that a student produces is wholly his own; it is more cyclical and requires more intuitive thought and feeling through which a student develops an inner trust. Through creative writing, dramatics, fine arts, music, even athletics, a student can find the means to explore what it is to depend on himself for success. It is vital for children to develop the realization that within themselves are myriad possibilities and potentials for completing a given task successfully and that they needn't always depend on a set standard of "right and wrong" for success.

Likewise, the whole idea that a student needn't necessarily memorize those things once thought of as common knowledge is an idea which has hopefully passed, and if it hasn't yet, we need to be sure that it goes by the wayside soon. There is that undisputable need for children to move into the world with the understanding of how to attain access to needed information, but it is of equal importance that they move into the world as well with the ability to call on their own minds and intellects in recalling information. To educate children that they can always depend on an outside source for needed knowledge or information is to do them a terrible disservice. Not only does it leave them weakened, the lack of self-reliance translates into other areas of their lives as well where they find themselves dependent upon outside sources and voices, and they may well "behave accurately with inaccurate information".

Finally, schools can reinstate, or maintain a balance between the work children are asked to do individually and in groups. This last seems important since so many of the educational trends today lean towards group process, collaborative teaming, cooperative learning or whatever name it is given. Just as there is merit in children's ability to be skilled in both accessing outside information and that within themselves, it is equally important for our children to not only be able to work effectively in groups but also to understand the importance of individual thought, not only to themselves, but also to their efficient functioning within a group.

LOST SOULS

Because so much of the emphasis today is on teamwork and working as a group, there has been a movement away from a balance between this and what might best be called individualism. While our popular culture has increased the emphasis in group teaming and decision making and has witnessed the resultant decrease in the recognition of the value of individuality, there are numerous examples throughout history of the contributions made by people who did not conform to popular thought. It is almost insulting to the intelligence to question what would have happened if Columbus, Newton, Galileo, Franklin, Edison, Einstein or any of the other great thinkers of their day had conformed to popular theory and thought and dismissed their inner voice. Indeed, all of these were misunderstood, questioned, disputed and even ridiculed at times, yet because they chose to follow their own path and were convinced of their beliefs and views they made great strides in their areas of thought and inquiry. Yet today in our society as well as in the classrooms housing our children, the trend is towards group thought, lessons and consensus. It truly is, for any of us, a difficult thing to be out of the mainstream, whether of popular thought or deed, and this is especially true for young people who have yet to develop the full measure of self-reliance that would allow them to act on their own with confidence. With the increase in cooperative grouping, there is less opportunity for them to develop the strength of self-trust. They tend to avoid "swimming upstream" and are more inclined to go along with the group. This impacts them not only within the classroom, but in all areas of their lives. With the current norms and ideas being promoted by their peer group, the media and others, the inability of our young people to be self-reliant and heed the voice of the soul is a very real concern. They may well end up as those rudderless ships who seek any port in a storm, no matter how detrimental it is to them or the world around them.

To provide for our children a solid balance between group work and individual time for work and reflection means allowing them the opportunity to see how their individual thoughts and ideas can take on a life of their own and develop into something powerful and strong. It allows them the chance to recognize the value and worth of their own mind and talents in developing strength in both knowledge and character. It enables them to be more assertive and confident in their interactions when they are in a group, so that they are not afraid to express differing opinions and beliefs so as to speak to those things that they believe are important. It further allows them the ability to soulfully evaluate the merits of those things the world around them works to convince them that they should be, do or have. And all of these things lead to greater self-reliance and a greater connection to the soul, which will perpetuate itself in shows of even more self-trust and wisdom.

With the benefits being so great for the students, the school community and the society at large, and the cost being from very small to nonexistent, only one question remains. Why would we think of doing other than providing avenues for our students to nurture and exercise and practice their self-reliance and the soulfulness that is intertwined?

CHAPTER 4

The Need to be Loved

The only thing I can vividly remember from the birth of each of my children was not the pain or discomfort of the labor, but of the overwhelming feeling that hit me as soon as I first laid eyes on them. Those tiny, helpless bits of humanity caused me an emotion so great as to leave me in speechless tears with an awe at the miracle of life and totally in love with these that had been created. As they have grown, this powerful emotional bond with the two of them has not diminished, but has strengthened. Though their dependency on me and their dad as a source of food, care, comfort and entertainment has greatly declined since their infancy, the fact that they have always known secure and stable sources of love and belonging has allowed them to become happy and content individuals, fully capable of sharing their love with those around them.

A lot has been researched and written about the need that humans have to be loved and cared for by others around them. Studies document the ill effects on infants who receive little or no touching following their birth. It is often noted how often an elderly person passes away shortly after the death of their life mate. Regardless of age, it is a human necessity to give and receive love. It is an emotion that not only impacts our physical health and well-being, but the health and well-being of our souls as well. This being the case, it is terribly sad that we live in a world where so many children are neglected in this so basic necessity.

LOVE AS A BUILDING BLOCK TO THE SOUL

Love and connection with other humans is a necessary component to the exercise, nurture and development of the soul and this is explained quite well when we remember that it is within the soul and through the soul that a human experiences the full gamut of emotions, perhaps none so strong or so overpowering than love. Through this emotion, we experience those moments of speechless awe and wonderment when we bring a child into the world; we feel the throat-tightening pride as we watch our children succeed in their endeavors; we establish bonds and connections with life-long mates. Through love, we recognize the desire and willingness to help, nurture and support other humans in the world around us and through love we develop the ability to sacrifice our own individual wants and desires for the good of someone else. Even the lows associated with the loss of love are necessary to the exercise of the soul, for as Jung notes in discussing the separation of one person from others, "However wretched this state may be, it also stands him in good stead, for in this way alone can he take his own measure and learn what an invaluable treasure is the love of his fellow-beings. It is, moreover, only in the state of complete abandonment and loneliness that we experience the helpful powers of our own natures."[1] This last is notable in that it indicates how even the loss of love can lead to a strengthening of that self-reliance previously noted as nurturing to the soul.

In the world at present, there is an apparent dismissal of the importance love has to the successful human experience and the development of a solid foundation of soul. The rate of child abuse has skyrocketed over the past few decades and those suffering are children who are without a well-founded base of love on which their soul can develop. Parents often work diligently outside of the home to the extent that their time to interact with their children is diminished, and the time for love and bonding between parents and children is likewise shortened. The children torn from their homes through bitter divorce have their beliefs and ideas about the nature of love irreparably damaged, forever changing their views. Whether through overt abuse, benign neglect or inappropriate life lessons, more and more children are entering the schools without that well-formed sense of love and belonging that is so necessary to their success and emotional foundation and well-being and within those schools and in the society at large, the results are being felt.

IT SHOULD HAVE NEVER HAPPENED

I have a hard time disliking any student. Perhaps because I have always considered any misbehavior or disciplinary problem the result of inappropriate or dysfunctional life-lessons, I always believed that within even the worst of children, there was some seed of inherent goodness that only needed to be cultivated and cared for in order to flourish into full-grown good. One student, however, seriously shook my belief in this and he is one that I'm not likely to ever forget.

It was early in my career as an assistant principal that I came into contact with Cal. He was a tall, slender young man of 16, with dark brown eyes and sandy brown hair cut short. He dressed in the usual teenage fashion of jeans, t-shirts and tennis shoes, and would remove the requisite baseball hat from his head whenever he entered the building. There was surely nothing to distinguish him from the hundreds of other students that moved through our halls on a daily basis, yet there was something about Cal that made it difficult for me to like him or to even believe that somewhere inside him was that seed of good that I thought was part and parcel of all children. In retrospect now, I realize that the primary reason that I felt so cool towards Cal was the fact that there was not one time during the numerous occasions that I had to discipline him on a school rule violation that I didn't feel like I was being manipulated or conned. He was just too smooth and glib to be believable.

Early on during his junior year, his transgressions in the school setting were fairly insignificant--skipping class, inappropriate language, disrespect towards authority. Each time he'd enter my office, he'd sit down and smile, apologizing profusely for his misstep and taking full responsibility for what he had done.

In November of that year, he was reported to have marijuana in a bag in his locker by a fellow student. I notified the principal and headed out into the building to conduct a search of his locker and his belongings. Cal was in a classroom near where his locker was located, so I went into the class and requested him to come into the hallway along with his teacher as a witness.

"I have reasonable cause to believe that you've got drugs in your locker, Cal." I told him. "Do you want to tell me what I'm going to find when I open it?"

For the first time, I noticed an anger in his eyes that I'd never seen in our earlier dealings. Gone was the benign look of ownership for misbehavior and in its place was a look that might best be described as hate.

"You have no goddam right to search my locker," he said in a low, hostile tone. "And you won't find anything."

I turned to the locker and opened it with the master key. Cal watched as I went through his coat pockets, book bag and other possessions. Nothing was found. I turned back to look at Cal, standing next to the teacher, the look of hate now replaced by one of vicious amusement. "I told you," he said smugly. "Why don't you go pick on someone else for once." He turned and went into the classroom and I headed back towards my office. I was sure that in some way, Cal had gotten rid of whatever he had stashed in his locker. The other student had just been too certain and too definite with the information. I returned to tell the principal that nothing had been found, and though he asked me who had given me the information, I told him that I had promised the student I would tell no one that he had reported the drugs to me, and felt I should honor that request. Agreeing, the principal said he, too, would keep his eye out and let me know if he heard of any other problems with Cal.

I got a phone call at home late that night. It was the mother of the student who had told me of the marijuana in Cal's locker. Her son was in the hospital, badly beaten by two or three people who had jumped him as he left his job in the mall that night. She knew that her son had told me about the problem with Cal. Was there, she pleaded in tears, any way that anyone else could have known that her boy had reported the drugs? "They don't know who did this," she cried. "But why else would anyone else want to hurt my son?"

I assured her that I had told no one, and went on to say that the way in which her son had reported the drugs in the locker was such that it would have been virtually impossible for anyone to have known he had done so.

The next day when I returned to school, I moved down the hall to where a group of students were gathered. In their midst was Cal, looking smug and self-satisfied and on a locker a short distance from where he stood, the word "Narc" had been written in large, bold print. I didn't need to know whose locker it was. But I did want to know how Cal had found out.

The next few weeks of school passed by fairly quietly. We kept our eye on Cal as much as possible, particularly when the assaulted student returned to school. But Cal stayed quiet and as free from obvious trouble and problems as he had ever been. I didn't understand it and didn't question it much, simply hoping that it was a sign of growth on his part. His father's visit to my office dismissed this notion.

Cal's dad had made an appointment to see me through my secretary, requesting that I not let Cal know that he was coming in. He came in on a bitterly cold, December morning, shortly after first hour classes had gotten underway. He seemed agitated and upset as I had him sit down.

Wasting no time with amenities, the father immediately launched into the reason for his visit. "I don't know if you've heard yet, but Cal's in some trouble with the police, the little S.O.B." he growled. " Seems he's taken to doing some cocaine, and stealin' to buy it. They tell me 'cause he's only sixteen, it's still my responsibility. If she'd take the kid, I'd send him back to his mom today, but she won't have a thing to do with him, especially with her new boyfriend." This last came out with bitter sarcasm, anger flashing in his eyes. "I thought you should know, since you've already searched him before. Maybe you should keep your eye out. The cops say that they doubt he'll be sent to jail or the juvenile home since its just his first offense."

I assured the father that I would, to the extent possible, keep my eye out and that as of that date, Cal appeared to be keeping out of trouble at school. I had gotten no more reports of drugs, nor had there been any other reported behavioral problems recently, yet I often wondered if the beating of the young man who had reported him previously had effectively educated other students that Cal was just not a person to mess around with. If such was the case, I soon learned that the students were probably correct.

Perhaps a week after the first visit, Cal's father was back in my office, unannounced and once again agitated and upset. He refused the seat offered, and remained pacing. "Cal's done it now. Cops got him last night for grand theft of an automobile. He probably won't be in school for a while. I think they've got him this time." He seemed more than relieved. He seemed pleased. Yet his forecast was not correct, and two days later, Cal was back in school, smug, self-satisfied. He seemed to revel in the glory of his crime and began to clearly illustrate the idea that he considered himself invincible, and his behavior in school deteriorated.

Shortly before spring recess that year, Cal had finally pushed the school rules too far. He had, in his apparent belief that he was beyond risk of punishment, begun a wholesale dismissal of school rules. He cut classes, smoked on school grounds, caused disruption in the classroom, got into fights and for all these he was suspended on a regular basis, with each progressive disciplinary proceeding leading to his dismissal from school. The final straw came when he reported to campus, having been absent for nine previous days. He was found in his car in the parking lot, reeking of marijuana and obviously under its influence. A plastic baggie was found in the glove box, filled with the drug. I remember that he laughed as he was ordered in to the school so that we could call the police and file a report, again displaying the arrogance that had marked his behavior in the past.

"This is it, I'm afraid," I told him. "You're at a point where we have no choice but to dismiss you from school." I went back through his past offenses, illustrating the progressive nature of the discipline. "Nothing we've been able to do or offer seems to have helped, Cal. I've no choice but to let you go until you can come into school and do what you're supposed to do."

I was struck again by the arrogance of his tone. "You can't do shit." he smirked. "I'll fight this and win. The pot isn't even mine."

I turned to the phone. "You'll have to explain that to your father and to the police." I said. "There's nothing more to say, other than I hope you wake up before its way too late. Prison's not a kind place and it seems as if that's the path you're choosing."

It was the last thing I ever said to Cal. We filed a police report and began the process to conduct an expulsion hearing. Having gone for arraignment on the charge of possession of marijuana, he was released to his father's custody, pending a hearing in juvenile courts. This hearing was never to occur.

A week later, just as schools dismissed for the break, we heard that Cal had disappeared from the area. While we didn't connect it immediately, at the same time, reports were coming in on another student, a female, who was missing from the area as well. Days later, her body was found, dumped by a roadside in Arizona. He, along with one of his friends, were located in California a short time later, in possession of her car--a car he had killed for.

Cal never made it to juvenile court. He was tried as an adult for murder and was sentenced to life in prison without parole. Sadly, witnesses to the trial commented later that, as he had appeared in school, Cal had moved through the trial and sentencing with no sign of remorse, only that same arrogance that had so marked his last few weeks of school.

———

Cal's story is an admittedly extreme case of a child who grows without a solid sense of love and belonging. His parents had divorced when he was very young. By the time he entered 6th grade, he had been enrolled in four different schools. Not only was bonding difficult given his home situation, his movement in and out of different schools precluded bonding for any length of time there as well. Not unlike any other child from a similar situation, Cal's cumulative record revealed an initial willingness to be cooperative and polite. In the early grades his records indicated a desire to please. There were notes in his file about his good manners and willingness to help other children and adults. Somewhere, though difficult to pinpoint exactly, he started to act up and out. In fifth grade, the term "sneaky" was appearing in the file. By his junior high years, the disciplinary problems had escalated, his grades were failing and he was displaying aggressive tendencies and a lack of remorse for his misbehavior. And by the time he reached high school, these tendencies and behaviors were so ingrained that any intervention or attempts to be proactive were of no use; there was left only the reactions to Cal's behavior. Since these only fit into the vicious circle that Cal was caught up in, and since he saw absolutely no need for creating a change, it was a circle that spiraled into the destruction of his life and another as well.

Though this is an extreme case, the number of children who similarly enter the schools without a well-developed sense of love and belonging often seems overwhelming, and they too often seek inappropriate, dangerous or destructive means to cement this needed part into the foundation of their soul. The tremendous increase in teenage pregnancy offers one verification of what happens when our young people seek to establish ties of love and belonging with another person. The rise in numbers of students who join gangs as well offers illustration of the desire to connect and fit in with other human beings. And on the extreme side, those like Cal at some point give up on trying to connect with others. These are those who have no emotional bond with the world or people around them. They display a lack of affect and a lack of remorse for their misdeeds or the harm that they cause to others. Their years of unsuccessfully bonding with anyone else in a meaningful way has severed their connection to their soul, and not only they, but also the world around them suffers the results.

LOVE AND BELONGING IN THE SCHOOLS

It is doubtful that anyone could or would argue that we are not suffering from a painful shortage of love in the world and in our society, particularly where our children are concerned. That this is most likely the logical outgrowth of a world that has grown so rapidly, and which has become more technological and less interpersonal is of note, but is not something that can be halted or even modified over night. What can be done is to develop an understanding and appreciation of just how necessary is the human need to love and be loved and to bond with other people and to work to assure that everyone has this opportunity in an appropriate way. Again, for those who work in the schools, the opportunities to provide for a measure of love and belonging are easy to find.

As our society has changed, schools are faced with those societal problems that come intertwined with it, but none is so insidious to the welfare of our children, and our future, as the disintegration of the family structure which too often upsets the sense of love and belonging for our children. Within the schools, we have a wide variety of students, some who have a well-established bond of love, some who have a certain degree of this basic need, and some who are wholly without any true, functional bonding with anyone else. As is the case with the need for self-reliance, or any of the other things that exercise and nurture the soul, regardless of the degree of love and belonging a child experiences outside of school, all will benefit from opportunities to connect with others and such opportunities, whether overt or not, are easily found within the school setting.

Though it may seem a paradox to the soul's need for self-reliance, the need for love and belonging is one that is attained easily in the schools through the blending of students into groups. As we look at those children who enter the schools as whole, balanced individuals, it is readily noted that these blend into the group situations rapidly and naturally. Again a circle, the children who move into school systems with a well-founded sense of love and belonging fit into the groups that are established in the schools, whether in the classroom settings or in extra-curricular group work through arts or athletics. Such activities offer a means for students to continue the very functional circle that they operate within. They have lived their lives to that point being cared for and find it easy to care for others; they naturally move into a group, where the behaviors they have learned to exhibit, such as being helpful, courteous and fun are reinforced, and so they remain within the group. The bonding they establish with the group makes the school setting enjoyable and their behavior perpetuates itself. Should one of their groups disband, they will move gracefully into another group, and develop new ties and bonding with its members. For this type of student, the school quite simply needs to do nothing more than maintain the opportunity for students to engage in the extra-curricular opportunities that are traditionally found there.

If we return for a moment to clarify the paradox between this need for group activities and the concept of the need for self-reliance, we should return as well to the need for balance. For these children, who have a well-developed sense of themselves and who we would consider whole, they are not dependent on the group, but rather interdependent with it. They are able to offer different views, opinions, ideas or suggestions without concern that they will be alienated. In this way, not only is their need to be self-reliant still in evidence, but as well they fear no loss of connection from the group will arise from a difference of opinion. They are balanced, and easily weigh out the value of the group process and group decisions with the wisdom of their inner voice. Their soul is nurtured through both the ability to be self-reliant and the ability to bond and connect with others.

For the children with a less than well-developed sense of love and belonging, the school's work is a bit more demanding, but not outside the realm of what it is already doing. Again, it calls upon the schools to maintain or establish functional group opportunities that meet the needs of these students, which can be done both in and outside of the classroom. To do otherwise allows for the very real possibility, if not the certainty, that they will either develop less than functional group opportunities on their own, or they will, as individuals without connection, sever their ties to the school society and eventually the general society and display the dysfunctional behaviors that so affect both them and the world around them.

Within the classroom setting, the child who is without a well-formed sense of belonging can quite easily be offered opportunities to work in groups that are formed of classmates of his or her choosing. Under the guidance of a teacher who is willing to understand that such children don't necessarily view things in the same way as the more functional student, group work can be structured in such a way that it is more meaningful to their lives. I think happily of a teacher within a building who recognized that she could reach the same course objectives in her English class with some of these students by teaming them up to study a unit on poetry. Fully realizing that their appreciation of Dickinson, Whitman, or any other poet to be studied was lacking, she taught the requisite terms and structures to the students as an entire group, and then in small groups allowed each to examine different types of poetry and prepare presentations. Students all chose their own group members and were guided in the selection of the type of poetry to examine. For the groups composed of students who traditionally did not blend into functional group situations, she allowed for an examination of various types of rock and rap music as a poetry style, with the students having the opportunity to listen to, analyze and assess the words of the music they enjoyed. Not only were course objectives met, she also allowed a greater degree of willingness for the students to participate with a group, thereby meeting their need for bonding with others in a functional, acceptable way. Had she done otherwise, she told me later, she was certain that the non-connected students might have joined assigned groups, but they would not have participated, would have remained alienated from the group and from the class at large, and may well have disrupted the process for the other students. What was more important, she reported that the students were so pleased and proud with what they had accomplished as a group, they had requested that they be allowed to choose their groups for future assignments, and to also have the opportunity to look at non-traditional ways for meeting course objectives. A wise teacher, she developed a trust among all her students through this, so that on those occasions when the traditional approach had to be followed, they did so willingly, knowing that at some point in the future they would be allowed to take alternate routes with groups of their choosing.

The idea of providing alternate roads for our students to participate with others within the schools extends beyond the classroom setting alone. For the child without a well-formed sense of love and belonging and who is not connected to the school setting in any way, many of the traditional extra-curriculars are and remain outside his or her realm of experience, and for this reason, developing alternative approaches and activities for this type of child serves not only the child well, but it also is in the best interest of the school. Because the need to connect with others is so necessary to the soul, it is not a need that can or will be circumvented. For the children lacking this, they will connect with others through those things noted earlier--gang activity, or sex, or partying--and will bring the associated problems with them into the schools. This is a given. For this reason, the schools are wise to explore what activities they can provide for that may meet these students need to connect with the school setting.

About four years ago, the realization that this type of student really was without the needed connection with others hit me hard. As the school disciplinarian, it was these students that were regularly coming into my office on discipline referrals. I was discouraged by the fact that almost without exception, those students who were our repeat offenders were those who fit a number of criteria. They generally came from a dysfunctional home situation. They rarely, if ever, participated in any extra-curricular activities. Their misdeeds were generally ones that caused disruption to the educational process within the classroom. And they saw little if any value in anything that the school had to teach them. Given all this, their attendance patterns were generally poor. Again, it was that vicious circle.

It occurred to me that teaming these students together into some type of group that was connected to the school might not be only advantageous to their chances for success, but to the school as well. Joining with some like-minded colleagues, we developed a plan to organize a group of these students and to take them to a camp for a week one summer to teach them team building, interpersonal and other life skills. We knew other school systems that took their "best and brightest" students to similar camps to teach leadership skills, but we believed that working with these, that we labeled as "high potential with low achievement" was equally, if not more, necessary. It seemed that those "best and brightest" would probably be fine, regardless of what we did or taught--they were already whole and well- balanced with a well-founded sense of love and belonging. These others, however, could not be disregarded and it only made sense to us to offer some avenue for them to not only learn strategies for success, but to do so as well while bonding with other students and school personnel.

Now into its fourth year, our U-Turn Team, as the first year's group named themselves, has become an established group within our school, regularly asked about by other students who hear about it and who want to join. And each year, we select a group of students who seem without connection to the school setting and who are generally without a well-formed sense of love and belonging anywhere in their lives. Together, we work to form into a team of adults and students who explore pathways and strategies for success, both within and outside of the school setting. I've never believed that it is the exploration of these paths or strategies that has allowed the students to achieve at a higher level than they did previously. Rather, it seems more the connection they have established with the group in a positive and productive way that has allowed them to truly make a "u-turn".

This brings up another point regarding this whole idea of love and belonging and connection and is one that I alluded to earlier perhaps in mentioning that this particular soul need is not only fostered in overt, clear-cut ways. Perhaps equally important is the non-visible means of establishing bonds of love and belonging and that comes through a wholly non-judgmental approach in working with the children who enter into our schools, a tough thing to sometimes accomplish.

Carl Jung wrote, "We can get in touch with another person only by an attitude of unprejudiced objectivity...It is a human quality--a kind of deep respect for facts and events and for the person who suffers from them--a respect for the secret of such a human life."[2] Yet though this is true, the ability to do so is a difficult thing indeed. Most of us have spent our lives judging people on their merits, abilities, attitudes and behaviors and have been similarly judged ourselves. If we step out of ourselves for a moment, and consider how it feels when we are the ones being judged, we can easily see how much discomfort this can cause, particularly if we are viewed harshly because our views or behaviors do not fit in with the mainstream of popular thought or convention. For children who enter the schools not fitting in with the commonly held perception of what a good student is or should be, judgments abound, starting in the earliest grades, from both the other children and the adults within the setting. For these children, school can rather rapidly become a place that they grow to hate and to rebel against, and those who work within the schools seek desperately to find a way to move students past this rebellion.

"We cannot change anything unless we accept it." Jung wrote. "Condemnation does not liberate, it oppresses. I am the oppressor of the person I condemn, not his friend and fellow-sufferer. I do not in the least mean to say that we must never pass judgment in the cases of persons whom we desire to help and improve. But...to help a human being...be able to accept him as he is."[3] That is what is most basic to what the non-connected child within the school setting needs. While the judgments and prejudices of fellow students are not something that can be wholly circumvented by the adults in a school, the adults themselves can learn to operate with that air of "unprejudiced objectivity" that Jung refers to, and model a non-judgmental approach for the other students. Not only is this seen in the acceptance of an alternate mode of dress, hair style, and appearance, but as well as in those activities that they may wish to engage in that are perhaps somewhat outside our traditional comfort levels. I think a group of students for example, who approached me prior to a school-wide activity day, in which students were going to have a variety of activities to participate in during the last two hours of a school day. Not finding their needs met in the volleyball, Euchre tournament, basketball, Trivial Pursuit or other offered activities, this group approached requesting that they be allowed to bring in their musical instruments and set up a mini "jam-session" in the courtyard of the school. They fully expected that their request would be denied, yet because they had requested so appropriately, the request was granted. I will testify that the music they played was not of the sort I nor the other adults in the building might listen to, yet to deny this opportunity would have been to pass judgment and thereby devalue those students and what they saw as important and valuable, and to do so would further assure a lessened sense of love and belonging and a lessened connection with the school.

There are a variety of like approaches that can be explored by those who work within the schools to provide for opportunities for students to team up with other children in what might not be traditionally seen as school-related opportunities. If a school is providing time for pep rallies and recognition of athletic teams, it is equally important to provide for non-traditional types of recognitions for other students. Allowing a band, such as the one that performed during our school's activity day, to perform at a basketball game or school dance is one example. Schools may note the increase in the number of students who, with incredible skill and prowess, engage in athletic activities such as skate boarding or rollerblading. While not a typical school event, providing opportunities for the students to participate or demonstrate during assemblies or activities illustrates an acceptance of those things that they find fun and valuable, and allows them to participate in them in an acceptable way, sanctioned by the school. Alternate avenues to work with course objectives can be allowed for, much as did the English teacher with her poetry lesson. By doing so, we educate the students that we are not judging their attitudes, their likes or their beliefs. Moreover, it educates both the non-traditional and traditional student alike that the adults who oversee such a large part of their lives are willing to work with them on the things that they enjoy and through this, students realize a greater sense of acceptance and work more willingly with those adults. A sense of love and belonging has a greater chance of being developed.

I can envision the concern and even the outrage of some skeptics who see this as a wholesale dismissal of the values and education that are important for children to have. If we are non-judgmental, doesn't that mean that we are opening ourselves up to accept things that are not at all acceptable? Doesn't that smack of the "do your own thing" mentality, with a lack of concern as to how "your own thing" might impact the others in the world around us? Again, the word is balance.

Being non-judgmental does not mean allowing for any type of behavior. It simply means not judging, and rather working with children with objectivity in order for them to develop trust and the realization that they are loved and accepted as a human being, regardless of their appearance, their attitudes or their likes and dislikes. It is only through such an approach that the opportunities to help that child will surface. Without it, we cannot hope to get close enough to provide these with the means to see for themselves which of their attitudes and behaviors truly serve them well.

There is a huge difference between being non-judgmental and accepting the varying types of dysfunction that children bring into the schools. It is the difference often seen between being empathetic and sympathetic. The adult who is empathetic is non-judgmental in approach and accepts the child where he is. Because the child does not feel devalued by being judged and senses that the adult is willing to understand, though not necessarily accept, his wants, needs, desires and attitudes, the avenues for the child to be guided to by this adult are greatly increased. It is more likely for the child in this situation to open up to that adult and to learn and grow in appropriate ways through their interaction. The beginning of a functional circle is set up.

For the adult who, with all good intentions, is sympathetic towards a child, too often may find that sympathy can lead to an acceptance of inappropriate behaviors or attitudes, based on the belief that it is not the child's "fault"; he is simply a product of his environment. This type of blaming serves no purpose and is, in and of itself, judgmental. It tends to assume that the child cannot be blamed, and cannot be expected to modify behaviors since he has been raised in a dysfunctional way. If a child is then enabled to continue with dysfunctional attitudes and behavior because there is an "excuse" for it, not only is his self-reliance curtailed, the ability to establish ties of love and belonging with others in the world will also be curtailed. There will be few places in the schools or in the world at large where such a person will find people who will be accepting of poor attitudes and behaviors, whether the circumstances of his life are known or not. Again a circle is either set up or perpetuated, this time of the most vicious of sorts, whereby the child feels unloved, acts out in inappropriate behavior, is excused for the misbehavior based on his upbringing, continues acting out, eventually discovers that others won't accept the behavior, which causes anger and frustration, which causes more acting out, and so the circle goes. Suffice it to say that it is important to distinguish between being empathetic towards a child and sympathetic.

Can the schools be the hope for students who are without a well-formed sense of love and belonging so important to the well-being of the soul? It is an important question. Truly there will be children who enter the school setting with a foundation so eroded from lack of love that it will be virtually impossible for the schools to do all the necessary repair work. Yet even the Cal's of this world, the most extreme cases, exhibit the tendency and desire to be loved and to love others during those early years. This little seed of goodness is what needs to be nurtured, tended and cared for, and the schools have the opportunity and the people who are able to do the cultivating. Providing all students with avenues to connect with others, both inside and outside of the classroom and in ways tailored to meet their individual needs and desires is one means of approach. Operating with all children in a caring, non-judgmental and empathetic approach is another step. Recognizing and appreciating their individuality, whether in appearance, beliefs, or likes and dislikes, and allowing for these to come into play within the school setting is yet one more. All of these are relatively simple, requiring little more than an acceptance that through these the children will have greater chance of realizing their need for love and belonging and through this both the school and the society stand to gain.

For those within the schools, having students who have a well-developed or a developing sense of love and belonging means that there will be less tendency to engage in the gang activity, the parties, or the adolescent sex that not only causes them problems as individuals, but which brings associated problems into the schools either directly or indirectly. It means that the students will feel less angry and hostile, and will, therefore, be less likely to act out in aggressive ways and disrupt the educational process. It allows the students to be more connected with the school setting, to display more positive attendance and behavior patterns, thereby allowing the adults who care for them there to have a greater impact and influence on their lives. Such a simple thing to do for so much gain.

For the community and the world around these children, there are like benefits. Children who have a solid sense of love, either through the home or through the school or through a combination of the two, are children who grow into the productive members of our society. Less likely to seek fulfillment of their need for love by becoming parents before they are ready, they become the adults who perpetuate a positive circle by parenting at the appropriate point in their lives and nurturing their offspring with a well-developed sense of love. Not focused solely on themselves, they are able to give to the others in the world around them. Because they know the connection and bonding with other people, they are less likely to engage in violence against others. All in all, they are less disassociated from the world at large and both they and the society around them stand to benefit.

THE NEED TO BE LOVED

CHAPTER 5

Offering the Soul Simplicity and Freedom

In a world that is, without question, increasingly difficult and complex, it should not come as a surprise that people are less happy and less satisfied than they once were. The soul's inherent need for simplicity and the freedom that results from it is a requirement that is less likely met. We return to the concept that for a given increase in one area, there is bound to be an associated decline in another and so as we consider the growth in the complexities of life, it would follow that there would be a corresponding decline in the opportunity to keep things simple. One more element that would provide for exercise and nurture to the souls of the inhabitants in our world loses out in the race to keep up in this elaborate and demanding world we have created.

The rise in technological advances is perhaps the single biggest factor in the increase in complexity of our world today for it is this that has served to provide us with the information as to what we should be, have or do and it is this that has likewise convinced us that complying with this information will bring happiness. Our growth in technology has provided us with the ability to access information at an ever faster rate, so that where we once had a great deal of time to gather, absorb and act upon information received, we now are able and often required to access, process and act upon information in mere moments. Combined with this, we have been allotted little time to learn the skills and strategies to do all of this effectively, and are left stranded in the awkward and uncomfortable position of often having to act on information as soon as it is received without the benefit of time for reflection and thought. Invariably, this leaves us in the position of having made decisions and realizing later that our actions resulting from these were not as sound or well-thought out as they might have been.

What this means in more concrete and familiar terms is that the outside voices that are so powerful in our world today have effectively achieved the goal of moving us to a point where we are busily trying to keep up with the world around us, whether in obtaining and maintaining the material things we are sure we should have, in behaving in one way or another as dictated by these voices, or in attempting to keep up with the status quo of the world around us. As the speed in which we do things increases, the simplicity of our lives decreases. We are constantly on the go, regularly overwhelmed by competing demands, and increasingly frustrated that there seems to be so little time in a day. We have become so preoccupied with all of this that there is, at best, only infrequent opportunities to stop or just slow down and appreciate the simplicity, freedom and meaning that life has to offer. As we feel our dissatisfaction mount under these circumstances, we can be sure that what we are feeling is the discontent of our souls.

For our children, the increase in complexity of the world around them is nothing more than another mark of the manner in which their childhood is being shortened with devastating consequences. All of those things that have been mentioned previously, the unhappiness, the dysfunction, the inappropriate behaviors and attitudes seen among too many young people are closely interwoven with the movement away from simplicity. What is equally notable and frightening is that just as much as the two aforementioned soul needs--self-reliance and love--the need for simplicity and freedom is one that when absent wreaks havoc on the souls of both the child raised in the most functional of homes and the one who has been raised in a less than functional environment.

A SIMPLE DEFINITION

So as to more clearly define what is meant here by simplicity and how it is intertwined with the associated soul need for freedom, it is probably most easily put that simplicity is the absence of those things that clutter our lives without adding true meaning to it. When we find life complicated by stressful jobs, expensive possessions that we need those stressful jobs to maintain, and a constant and hectic speed and pace that burdens us with even more stress, we can safely say that we have dismissed simplicity from our lives. In doing so, we also find that there is less time for us to feel free from the pressures, demands and expectations of those around us. Constantly on the go, constantly busy and constantly unable to simply sit back and enjoy the interaction and connection with the important people in our lives, it is no surprise that we are unhappy. Life is too complex. Those who maintain simplicity are those who have learned to balance the demands of the world with the need of their souls for the time to be quiet and enjoy a slower pace of life. In order to keep things simple, these people carefully evaluate the information and demands that constantly vie for attention. They weigh the merits and value of those things suggested and resist feeling pressured to do, say, or be anything that would complicate their life or restrict their freedom. A person operating with a measure of simplicity is noted by a marked ability to remain free from stress and to maintain a positive attitude and outlook on life. They are never too busy or too stressed to simply look around and appreciate all the things that the world readily and freely has to offer.

For our children, and for those who work with them in the schools, it is important to realize that fewer and fewer of them, regardless of home situations, are seeing the world as simply as it might be seen. The most important teachers in their lives prior to entering school, both the parents and the outside voices of the media have been readily teaching them that keeping up with the demands of our technological and ever changing world is what they must be prepared for. Fewer of the children entering the schools of America will have had the opportunity to learn how to sort through the voices and the demands that press upon them and will have had even less opportunity to learn how to assess the value of these voices and demands. Because this simplicity and the freedom that is intertwined is so crucial to the exercise and development of a healthy soul, it is important that our schools offer a refuge to childhood and the simplicity that is inherent there.

THE OVER-ACHIEVER

Jenny came from a fine family. The middle child of three, she was by all definitions the example of an achiever. There was nothing that we knew of that she didn't do well. Whether math, social studies or English, Jenny breezed through them all. A straight-A student from her earliest grades, by high school, she was enrolled in the advanced placement classes and had even tested out of some, so that by the fall of her senior year, she had completed all offered science classes at the high school and had enrolled in some more advanced ones offered at the local community college. She, her parents and her school guidance counselor were certain that she would move on to a large, prestigious university upon graduation with full scholarship so that she could begin work on a degree in premed.

In January, just before the second semester of her senior year had begun, I was talking with Jenny's guidance counselor about some scheduling ideas when a teacher came into the office and asked to speak with both of us. "I'm concerned about Jenny Adams," he said. "She seems to kind of be struggling in my class and it seems out of character for her. Would you have time to see her?" The counselor nodded that she would, without question, get Jenny down to the office as soon as possible.

"I've been worrying about this," the counselor remarked to me as the teacher left the office. "Lately Jenny's been looking pretty stressed and unhappy, and though I've meant to talk with her, I just haven't gotten around to it."

"What's up with her?" I questioned. "She's going to be in the top ten of the class, she certainly has plenty of friends and is well thought of by everyone. Maybe just a case of 'senioritis'?" I smiled, knowing full well how many seniors got caught up in the competing demands of work and fun during their final year of high school.

"I think its more serious than that," she said. "Jenny's been pushing herself way too hard for four years, and its been an even harder push this year with attending the community college in the mornings before coming here. Combine this with her parents overriding desire to see her safely placed in a nice prestigious Big Ten school with a healthy scholarship behind her and I'd say the pressure is getting to her." She smiled. "She's such a nice kid, I'd hate to see her burn out here in the final months of school. She should be having time for fun and being a kid, but I don't think she or her parents are allowing for that. I'll be sure and see her."

A week later I happened to be in the counseling office when Jenny emerged from her counselor's office, looking angry and agitated. I peered into the office to see the counselor shaking her head from side to side in apparent resignation.

"It didn't go well with Jenny?" I asked, to which she motioned me to come inside and close the office door.

"I'm starting to get seriously concerned," the counselor said sadly. "I talked to her the same day the teacher asked me to and she just brushed off our concern, saying she was just fine; that she was really busy but she could manage it okay." Yesterday, that same teacher came back in and told me that he had caught her cheating on a test, and that her grades were slipping badly because she had failed to turn in a number of assignments. In English!" she said in amazement. "She's always excelled   in English!"

"So can you tell me what happened?" I asked. "She looked really angry when she left here."

I caught a glimmer of tears in the counselor's eye. "She told me to mind my own business. That she would pull the grade up, she'd just gotten too busy and had missed turning in some of the work, but she'd get it in." Looking resigned, she continued. "We've always gotten along well, but today she told me to leave her alone. 'You're not my mother', she told me. I was so surprised by the anger and the hostility, I didn't know what to say. It just caught me off guard."

The incident left its mark on the counselor and she did as requested, stepping back and letting Jenny continue on her chosen path towards graduation. Early in the final semester of the senior year, Jenny began to slip further. Her parents reported to the counselor that she had failed one of the courses at the community college the previous semester and was re-taking it along with another night class for the new semester. With this information, the counselor expressed her concern that Jenny might be biting off way too much for the final semester of her senior year and questioned whether the parents might want to look at the means to simplify things for her. Would they consider dropping one of the college courses or at least changing her high school schedule into one that was a bit less challenging than the totally advanced placed academic track she was on for this final semester?

Absolutely not, the parents had insisted. A demanding schedule will build character. After all, she will need to work at least this hard in a pre-med program. "She recognizes that she needs to sacrifice a little to get where she wants to be," her father had told the counselor. "She'll be just fine."

But she wasn't. By March of her senior year, Jenny, one of the best and brightest, had plummeted in both grades and in attitude. Her appearance was one that radiated stress coupled with anger and hostility. She was frequently short with others where she had once been pleasant. Assignments were not completed and if they were they were absent the quality that had always marked her work. By April, her attendance had deteriorated in part due to a bout with the flu and in part due to a depression that seemed to be permeating her whole being.

In May, her parents were meeting with the counselor. Jenny was refusing to return to school and nothing they could do could convince her to do otherwise. The parents were crying and distraught, questioning the counselor on how their daughter could do this to herself and to them. As the counselor brought in the papers to be signed identifying Jenny as a "drop", the counselor only questioned me as to how we, as a school, could have allowed this to happen.

It is not solely within the schools where we educate students away from the value and merits of simplicity, for as noted, our increasingly technological and complicated society has had a tremendous impact, often long before children even enter the world of public education. Taught through the media and possibly the home that the world they are moving into is one in which "keeping up with the Jones'" is the norm and that life is inherently fast-paced and hectic to this end, when they do enter the schools, this belief is reinforced. Children learn much more than just the educational material around them; they also pick up and learn attitudes, behaviors and beliefs modeled by those around them. Within the world of education and the prevailing mind set there, so closely aligned with the prevailing mind set of the world at large, they come to understand that learning itself is a difficult, complex and demanding task, and so see the educational material as difficult, complex and demanding. They are not inaccurate in this view, as more and more, the work they are being asked to do is precisely all these things.

For students such as Jenny, they may enter the world of education directly from a well-established, functional home situation. They may have all of the advantages that their parents can offer and may have access to the soul developing and nurturing opportunities for self-reliance and love. But equally essential to the soul is times for their lives to be simple and free. These students often concern me because they so readily fit into the world around them and comply so well with the demands that it places upon them to be high achievers. They are viewed as such by both the world at large, as well as by their parents and those who teach them in the schools. Surely it is the rare teacher that does not overwhelmingly prefer to have this type of student within the classroom, as they assure the teacher a much greater feeling of success than that found through work with the lower achieving student. But being put upon such a pedestal has tremendous disadvantages associated with the increased demands that invariably follow. Once again, a circle is set up. In this circle, the student achieves well, is praised and reinforced and is expected to continue at the current level or at a higher one. This in turn creates increased expectations that the student feels duty bound to meet. The vicious nature of this particular circle may be one that the high achieving student is as powerless to break as is the student caught in a vicious circle of misbehavior. Lacking the ability or willingness to do less than the real or perceived expectations of the significant people in their lives, or to do less than their own self-imposed expectations, such students are almost certain to be too busy to see the value of simplicity and freedom and how beneficial that is to their soul.

The complexity of the world both within and outside of the walls of education is equally damaging to the lower achieving student. They too are faced with an education as to what you should do, have or be in order to be measured as worthwhile. Prestigious, well-paying jobs, expensive cars and clothes and assorted possessions are equated with happiness and success and that with a good education, all of these can be theirs. The education of the world is often one that illustrates inaccurately that if you are without such things your life is not as good as it could be. For children in their formative years, this is a damaging lesson. These children, many of whom are also minus the self-reliance and love that nurtures the soul, enter an educational world where more and more the standards are being raised before they can meet the previous ones. As education steps up its emphasis in teaching primarily in the areas that are intellectual, linear-sequential and logical and decreases the emphasis in the more creative areas that provide for a measure of simplicity, the complex nature of these children's lives is intensified and their ability to find areas for success within the school is diminished. When this is coupled with the life lessons that they have learned as to what it takes to be successful, their seeming inability to meet these standards leaves them in a situation where they believe they just can't win. Not only do they feel as if they can't achieve in the educational setting, there is the associated frustration that is borne out of the connected belief that they will not be able to attain those things that they have been taught will make them happy.

That the schools have increased the demands they place upon students is not a surprise to anyone since they have done as they always have and followed the societal trends. They have blended the complexity of our increasingly technological world into the school setting in the course work and requirements for students and have likewise succumbed to outside voices and pressure to teach a variety of other things that once fell well outside of their realm. Because schools are recognized, as noted earlier, as being that one place where we can be sure that virtually all children will attend at one time or another, a wide range of teaching responsibilities has fallen within their domain. Teaching all those things noted in Chapter 2, such as sex education, cultural diversity, conflict resolution, AIDS awareness and the multitude of other things may be necessary and beneficial, yet it also serves to complicate and intensify the work of education and in turn complicate the lives of children. We recognize the value and validity in educating children on these issues and we recognize that the schools are a logical place to teach them, but as schools are more and more called upon to address a wide range of real and perceived issues, they are further and further moved from the days of reading, writing and arithmetic. And the students within those schools are moved further and further from that simplicity as well. The axiom can be observed in reverse here as we recognize that as education has decreased the simplicity with which they operate, they have seen a tremendous increase in the number of unhappy, dissatisfied and problematic students who are attending, or not attending American schools.

THE WISDOM OF SIMPLICITY

A colleague offered me a favorite quote one day as we were discussing the complicated nature of the world of education. "While intelligent people can often simplify the complex," he quoted, "A fool is more likely to complicate the simple".[1] Suffice it to say, he is one of the few educators I know that sees the inherent value in maintaining a degree of simplicity and freedom for our students and who likewise sees the harm in complicating and restricting them. Since the need for simplicity and freedom is one more need in assuring a solid foundation of soul, it seems important that the schools find the means to do as he suggested, simplify the complex rather than complicating the simple. The question to be answered is whether this is as easy in practice as it sounds.

The first exposure that children have to the world of public education is in the elementary schools when they are still in that formative stage of development and where they quite naturally operate with a measure of simplicity and freedom that is an inherent part of that stage of life. At these levels, it is the responsibility and the duty of the decision makers to begin to view the societal demands being placed upon them with a more objective eye, looking for what will be lessened if they follow the latest trend. It may well mean a reduction in natural simplicity and freedom. If they recognize and value the soul as an essential part of the children under their care, it is possible and even probable that they will recognize that many of these demands will serve to complicate the students' educational day. Given this realization, they will be better equipped to make an appropriate decision as to whether the demand should be met or not.

Consider an example. Suppose the latest push from a community is for the local elementary school to use a certain amount of its budgeted money for capital expenditures to purchase the newest computers and software available. The idea receives enthusiastic support as people believe students will be able to keep up with or move ahead of their counterparts in other schools or countries. What's more, such technology brings with it access to a host of other opportunities through on-line services such as the Internet or the World-Wide Web. Just imagine, say supporters, of the potentials available to children. True enough. On the surface, it seems like a credible thing to do and who would want to deny this to children if the opportunity were there? The educator who moves beyond just the surface potential will be wise to consider the hidden potentials as well and will see that there are not just potentials, but pitfalls too. What hidden costs will suddenly become visible when all of this technology comes into the schools? And how will all of those hidden expenses be paid, and what may not, therefore, be funded? During the average seven hours that a student is within the school, what time will be allotted for training and usage of these computers and the related technology and what parts of the childrens' day will have to be sacrificed in order to conduct this teaching? How much time will the average teacher lose from the classroom and from connecting with students in order that he or she can be effectively trained in their use? Will such use shorten or even preclude a child's time for working through their lessons and assignments in simple, basic ways?

If in answering such questions, the decision-makers within the schools determine that those problems can be addressed if the twice-a-week time for art is shortened to once a week, or that the music program could truly be implemented effectively as an after-school activity, or that time for recess or physical education can be shortened somewhat, then those decision-makers are without the recognition and appreciation of how important simplicity and freedom are to the childhood and the souls of the students they serve. Instead, they have effectively leaned towards complicating what should be simple and have moved with the societal winds that blow strongly towards educating children in complex, and often restricting ways--all at a high cost to the soul.

It must be noted here that such technology as well as the other ideas and demands that are finding their way into the schools are often credible and valuable. It returns again to the concept of balance. If the simple things of the elementary schools, such as music and art, recess and physical education are the things that get lost or are diminished as is so often the case, it behooves both the schools and the students to seek a balance. Is there a way for the technology or the innovation to be started on a smaller, simpler scale, that provides it as an opportunity for those who want to take advantage of it, while not impeding or shortening the time available for the more simple things? Is there a different level of education where such implementation not only has less of an impact on the students' time, but is also more developmentally appropriate? Is it truly a need for children, or is it one more equivalent of keeping up with the Jones' and heeding the outside voices of the world, thereby effectively stripping away more of the time of childhood and its simplicity and freedom already so curtailed by the world around us?

Once educators consider these and similar questions, they are likely, if they place any value of the soul-nurturing benefits of simplicity and freedom, to avoid rushing into such decisions quickly. Likewise, this careful consideration allows them the opportunity to develop a solid, rational argument that seeks to defend the childhood of their students against those things proposed that would effectively diminish it. It is only through a strong belief in and a strong defense of that simplicity necessary to childhood that it will be maintained.

It is a fairly safe assumption that many if not most of the elementary schools throughout the country are flirting with the inclusion of technology in either a large or small way or somewhere in between and no one, myself included, would suggest a wholesale dismissal of the time, money and effort which has been expended in integrating such technology into the classrooms. At the risk of being redundant, again the word is balance. For children in these classrooms to have opportunity to engage in simple, soul-nurturing activities, they have to be left time to work without the aid of a good software package that instructs them in how to complete a task. They need to be assured of the time to work with their own thoughts and ideas that come solely from within themselves, to struggle with the paper and pencil and eraser and end up with a product that is simple and uncomplicated, wholly their creation, misspellings and all. Their artwork may be more palatable by adult standards if it is created via a painting program on the computer, yet it will lack the soul-strengthening simplicity that comes out of pulling the creation totally from within themselves, transferring it from their mind and heart and soul, onto the paper in front of them. With such opportunities left intact and well-provided for in terms of time allotment, even with a computer in the classroom, the teacher will find that the students are learning the most and are the happiest when they are not only able to develop and work on a project through the wonders of modern technology, but when they have an appreciation of the simple ways to accomplish things of value as well.

It is not only the inclusion of technology within the elementary schools that serves to devalue the simple things, but also the rising tide of public demand for higher test scores, particularly in the areas that are linear and logical, such as math and science. The demands for improvements in these areas are understandable and well-intended again, if one believes that the best we can do for children, regardless of the level they are at, is to prepare them for the global competition and increasing complexity of the world that they will someday face. As in any other area, it always seems that when something seems very logical on the surface, it is probably wise to scratch that surface and see what lies beneath. In this case, what is found again is a picture of schools that emphasize improvements in test scores in mathematics and science and de-emphasize the value and simplicity found in the creative areas. In many states, school funding is tied into test score improvements and alignment with suggested or demanded core curriculums, and schools comply with this subtle blackmail willingly--and mistakenly. This is one more area which allows for dismissal of the simplicity necessary to childhood and the development of the soul. In the short term, it may seem that we are doing both the schools and the students a service, but in reality what we are doing is a grave disservice to the souls of our children and the schools in turn are, as noted, adversely impacted.

In answering the question then as to how schools can accomplish all that they are being asked to do and still find the means to keep at least some measure of simplicity and freedom for students, the simple answer for those within the elementary schools is to maintain this level of education as one where the students can be what they are by nature--children. They will have the time to learn all that they need to know to become efficient and effective members of the community in good time. Their opportunities to color and play, to sing and to dance, to invent games and songs and stories that are wholly their own, if maintained and encouraged will provide the soul the simplicity and freedom it needs. When this is coupled with the approval, love and encouragement from the adults who shepherd them through the schools, all of the soul nurturing components identified up until now--self-reliance, love, simplicity and freedom--will be in place. These children will find that learning is fun and enjoyable and they will more readily take to the other subjects provided to them by the school as well.

While the movement seen in today's elementary schools is towards the intellectual, logical, practical and complex, it is seen to an even greater extent within the secondary schools of America where educators find themselves with the unenviable task of getting their students ready for the world that they will enter and to do so effectively in a six to seven year time span. No wonder the heat feels like it is being applied full strength. It is. Those children who move through the elementary schools move into the normally complicated world of adolescence and the secondary schools where they find themselves facing increasing demands to become more intellectually and technologically competent. At this level, credits are more specific and the failure to succeed in a required class results in the need to repeat that course or another in the same area in order to move forward. The result of this tends to be that those children who find themselves repeating classes to have less opportunity to enroll in classes that may offer more simple pathways to success. Since these tend to be those students who are not all that fond of school anyway, their dislike grows as their school hours are increasingly complicated by curricular requirements that they struggle with and don't enjoy.

Now many of my colleagues and others who see the importance in educating our children to be ready to move into the complex world of work often simply adopt an attitude that says, in effect, "Then those students should just work harder and do better and then they'll not have to repeat classes and can take the classes that will provide for simplicity and freedom and all those other things." This may be a valid point and in an ideal world that might be exactly what such students would do. But as the curricular requirements for secondary school students across this country have been tightened up and complicated further, those who have always had a tough time now have it tougher. More and more students are coming through elementary systems where their opportunities for simplicity have been curtailed. Though our elementary schools were once the part of the school matrix that was marked by nurturing and empathy on the part of the teachers and other school personnel, this is less often the case as the complexity level of subject matter and day to day issues at the elementary grades continues to increase. This being the case, many students may well enter the secondary grades not overly fond of school, and the simple words of wisdom to "try harder" have no meaning. They are so disillusioned with not being able to move past the complicated and difficult tasks they are given, that they scoff at the possibility of trying harder. It is but another vicious circle being established, and the schools that fail to recognize the damage done by over-doing the complexity with which students are burdened often solidify and intensify these students' alienation from the school by continuing to increase standards and requirements. All too often, the students caught in this circle break out of it by simplifying their lives and dropping out.

For students such as Jenny who achieve at the level expected, the increase in complexity only furthers the pressure they face to keep up with what is asked of them. As the curricular standards are raised, these who have always performed above the standard feel pressure to perform at a higher level yet. Their lives become increasingly complicated with the stress of taking the higher level classes and performing well both in these and in the extra-curricular areas where they are also well-known for their achievement. These are moved further and further away from what it is to operate with a measure of simplicity and freedom; the hectic pace of their life precludes it. And though they may reach and exceed the real or imposed standards set, the increase in complexity and decrease in simplicity and freedom adversely impacts their overall happiness and the well-being of their souls. They may not follow their lower-achieving counterparts and drop out of the school setting, but they regularly are found to display a dissatisfaction and an unhappiness that comes from the regular stress felt from the complexity that so marks their lives.

I often hear the comment around colleagues about the "young adults" that we are working with in the secondary schools. I cringed at one recent meeting where we were told that we could work towards "de-juvenilizing" the high school and make it more adult. I literally had to hold back tears, as this comment was met with massive approval and support. My thoughts focused on the fact that we were working with juveniles, not adults. Yet here was one more term that illustrated the trend towards shortening childhood and increasing its complexity. Such terms are revealing as they speak to how the adults within the schools and community view the children who walk into the secondary halls and classrooms at the ripe old age of 12 or 13 and progress through the system by the time they're 17 or 18. These are still children and to view them as "young adults" may seem harmless enough, but remains harmless only if it doesn't color our views as to what the students are, what they need and how much complexity they should be required to handle. What they are is children who need the opportunity to develop at an appropriate pace for themselves as individuals, and to do so while maintaining a measure of simplicity and appreciation of the connected freedom. They further need the adults who are there to work with them to remember that each step along the way to true, whole adulthood is a small incremental one that cannot be rushed or complicated without doing harm to the soul.

For the secondary schools to maintain a level of simplicity and freedom for its students is not outside the realm of possibility if they, like their elementary counterparts, recognize the value of balance. It is interesting to note that in the past ten years or so, American schools, while maintaining, for example, a 22 credit requirement for graduation, have increased the average number of credits needed in math from two credits to three, and in science, from one credit to two. Likewise, within the last ten years, computer literacy or programming has appeared on more and more lists of graduation requirements. It doesn't take a mathematician to determine that if the requirements have remained at 22 credits and certain areas have seen an increase in needed credits, something has had to give. It doesn't take a genius to figure out what has lost out either. You need only assess those winds of change that are blowing towards the logical, practical, work-related and complex, and away from the intuitive, creative and simple. While this has been dictated by some very powerful outside forces and voices, educators are still considered to be the experts on what is best for the children they teach and therefore need to become a more active voice in favor of them and in favor of maintaining some soul-nurturing simplicity for their students. This means thoughtful questioning prior to adding one more curricular requirement to the load currently imposed upon students. Will it mean that all students, regardless of performance level, will have less opportunity to enroll in elective classes that might make their school day more meaningful and enjoyable? How will this impact those currently experiencing success and those who are not as successful? Will it result in increased pressure for the high achievers to achieve at an even higher level despite the associated increase in stress and dissatisfaction? Will it effectively raise the level of complexity to one that the lower achieving student feels powerless to overcome? And if the result for all is potentially less than favorable, then what is the true benefit in doing it? Where will the avenues for simplicity and freedom be paved if the curricular changes limit the current routes that students are able to find? What opportunities will still be available for the students to work with their intuitive and creative thought processes? Will we, by curtailing students access to the simple, the fun and the freedom and the soul-nurturing found there, be pushing them faster than those small steps of childhood and adolescence should truly be taken if one is to develop into a whole and happy adult?

It is questions like these, when considered at both the elementary and secondary levels, that can offer educators the ability to critically assess which curricular changes, technological advances and educational trends are actually improvements in the lives of their students. Through such questions and the resultant discussions and avenues of exploration, educators can better evaluate what they are doing, what they are being asked to add or change, and what is likely to result in terms of the impact on all of the students they work with, both those currently successful and those who are not. If, through this questioning, they determine that they are pushing children more quickly into the complex world of adulthood than developmentally appropriate, they must be wise enough to step back and reassess if they are allowing for a complication of the simple rather than a simplification of the complex and what the result of this will be for their students.

I remember speaking at length a few years ago with a student named Jimmy who was teetering between remaining in school or dropping out. The product of a dysfunctional home where the parents sought to place him squarely in the middle of their conflicts, he found school, like his home, a place where he would just rather not be. In talking with him, I was struck by how pointless he viewed all of those things that he was being asked to do within the school setting. "I think school is just a waste of my time," he responded to my question as to why he was considering dropping out. "Think about it." he said. "We learn a bunch of stuff that is supposed to get us a job. So we get into a job we don't like, and we work to make money, go home, go to bed and get up and do it all over again. What's the point?" he questioned finally. At that point in time, all of the outside voices that had been so effectively programmed into my brain kicked in and I found myself speaking to him on the value of work and how he'd appreciate a good education later. I offered the same educational jargon in defense of the schools that I'd been taught through all of my own schooling--that it may not seem valuable now, but he'd understand it better when he grew up. He just had to trust us.

Shortly thereafter and many times since, I returned to that conversation and similar ones that have taken place in my office and realized that what I had offered to Jimmy and to other students who found themselves unhappy with the complex nature of their schooling and in doubt of its value, was nothing more than quotations from the outside voices of this world which had convinced me that what students needed was to become efficient members of the community that they would enter. I assessed the discomfort I had always felt when saying such things to students and recognized that this uneasiness resulted from the fact that within my heart and soul, I didn't believe what I was saying. I was watching the educational community move children away from the natural simplicity and freedom of childhood and fill them with things that, at this stage of their life, were too complex, in which they saw little value and which caused them an unhappiness and discomfort that they could not effectively define. I knew that they were still in the process of taking those baby steps along the road to adulthood and were being pushed to take them in strides instead of small steps. It was clear that they watched the world around them through their friends and through the media and believed that everyone else was doing fine along the road, yet they were still dissatisfied and unhappy and unable to explain why. And here I was, doing nothing to help them clarify their confusion, rather offering them the standard adult wisdom, "We know what's best for you." This never served to benefit the students, nor did it offer them clarity or relief from their confusion; it only placed me in a position of most of the other adults in their lives, pushing them to speed up those steps and move more quickly into adulthood and economic efficiency.

But childhood is the time where the establishment and development of the soul takes place. Those of us who have reached adulthood are often tremendously guilty of forgetting that each step along the way of any journey needs to be undertaken slowly and appropriately and to rush any of the steps is to do disservice to the passage. Because we have forgotten this, or perhaps simply disregard its importance, we are that much more likely to encourage the adult-like skills and complexities to be developed and accepted at ever younger ages.

Benjamin Hoff comments on this in *The Te of Piglet* when he writes, "Rather than help children develop the abilities needed to overcome the difficulties immediately confronting them, in the natural order in which they need to develop them, the Eeyore Educational System (with a good deal of help from parents and the entertainment industry) is forcing too much inappropriate information on them too soon, concerning--and causing-- problems they can do nothing about. Then the children get stuck."[2] This last is understandable. Our children are being given too many complex learnings and lessons and in the process are short-changed or rushed through those developmentally appropriate steps so that they can more rapidly become adults capable of effective functioning. Yet in doing so, we effectively educate them that this world is full of complexity and short on simplicity and freedom, so there may well be a tendency to get stuck, cling to or revert to those stages that were not given the justice they deserved. This is not only due to a desire to regain what was missed of childhood, it is as well an effort to regain the connection with the soul and the simplicity and freedom it so craves.

CHAPTER 6

Creativity, Beauty and the Soul

The opportunity to create is a necessity to the soul for its exercise and health. If you consider the Biblical account of creation, and take into account the sixth day when God created man, you will recall that the story speaks to man being created in God's image. If, regardless of religious beliefs or leanings, you accept the concept that God created man in His own image, then it would follow that we would be, like our maker, creative and creating beings, and we are precisely that. No matter where you look in our world, you will find people in the act of creating. They are creating a multitude of things, including positive creations such as strong families, music, poetry, literature, art, new inventions, businesses and a list that could go on and on. Other creations are in process as well, including dysfunctional families, graffiti, violence, destruction, personal hardship, environmental disasters and again, an extensive list. No matter where you look or who you observe, you will see that all of us have a need to create. The question centers around whether what is being created is positive or negative and once again, this question centers around whether or not the person who is doing the creating is in touch with the soul.

Within any given school educators will attest to the fact that it often seems as if their student body is divided into groups, one which seems to excel within the setting, one which seems destined to not only fail but also drag others down in the process, and then those who fall somewhere between these two extremes. In considering these in terms of what each group is creating, those who excel have the means for and know the avenues to positive creativity. These students participate in activities such as athletics, theater, forensics and debate, art clubs, creative writing and a variety of curricular and extra-curricular offerings that afford the chance to create in positive ways.

The students at the opposite end of the spectrum, who are failing and withdrawing, are not connected to the school setting in any way that encourages them to create in positive ways. They have failed classes in the past and, because they need to atone for this by repeating curricular requirements, their opportunity for those courses where creativity is an integral part is severely limited. Yet these students still have a need to create and this they do. Their failure within the school setting diminishes the chance that they will be involved in school-sponsored extra-curricular activities, so they find the means to create through non-traditional appearances, through graffiti, through destruction, and through classroom disruptions. They may create personal hardships, dramas, and self-defeating behaviors that further preclude and prevent their success.

For the groups in between, some find means to connect, at least periodically, with the school setting and may find the means to create positively, but are equally likely to find ways to develop negative creations. Whether for these or either of the other groups, the need for creativity is not one which can be sidestepped or ignored and, as with the other soul nurturing needs, providing the opportunities for our students to find ways to exercise their creative potential, and thereby their souls, is in the best interest of the students, the school and the community at large.

CREATIVITY AND BEAUTY:
FOOD FOR THE SOUL

Creativity might best be defined as the need, desire and ability to produce something that is wholly your own, and perhaps this is precisely why it is such an important element to the strengthening of the soul. In the process of creation we are able to further strengthen the previously mentioned soul-needs as well. Through the creative process, we develop something that is of our own making, drawing on our own inner thoughts and strengths for its production, thereby enhancing our ability to be self-reliant. In order to create something of beauty, we need not utilize any complicated techniques or technologies, and can work with a measure of freedom and simplicity. Through successful creation we experience a swell of pride and pleasure in what has been accomplished and this feeling is one that we want to repeat. Whether we create in tandem with others or share our creativity with those around us, we find the opportunity to experience a sense of love and belonging. Truly the creative process is one that feeds and strengthens the soul.

As time goes on, our society moves further and further towards reliance and faith in things that are logical, scientific, technologically advanced and complicated, and the importance and value of creativity is dismissed as having a lessened importance. Less emphasis is given to this soul-need in the world at large, in the homes we live in and in the schools our children attend. For the children who are growing up in homes where the benefits of creativity are recognized, there is a greater chance that they will grow into positive creators. In their homes, they are offered opportunities to explore and create through finger-painting and silly songs, through imaginative play and family outings. Time is allotted for these so that such children are not kept so busy that they miss out on opportunities to develop their creative potentials. These will grow into the adults who recognize the need and have the ability to create in positive ways.

For a growing number of people there is less capacity for positive creation. Likely raised in homes where no emphasis is placed on the importance of having the time to be creative, these have little or no experience with that heart-swelling pride that comes through producing something of beauty. Though this may lie atrophied and dormant, this need of the soul still makes itself felt and the type of creativity among this group is very different from the other. For such children, often raised by the television as their baby-sitter, entertainer and educator, they learn to create similar dramas to those they watch. Some of these will create hardship for themselves by creating hardship for others through violence, abuse, neglect or greed, causing them even greater difficulties and problems. And if these fail to learn the benefits of positive creation, another circle will be set up in which these, so disassociated from the soul and the strengths to be had there, will begin the cycle anew with the children that they are entrusted to teach.

A TALE OF TWO CREATORS

Alissa and Laura entered high school the same year and along with that, had many other similar characteristics. Both were average in height, weight and appearance. Socioeconomic backgrounds were similar with both girls coming from typical, middle class homes. Both were average in their academic abilities, with test scores and other measures indicating the need to work hard in order to achieve at specified levels. Each seemed well accepted by their peer group, and as they entered their freshman year at the high school, each was enrolled in a fairly typical schedule of classes for a ninth grade student. In fact, in looking at their schedules, only one thing was different. Alissa had opted for a first-year arts and crafts course as well as choir while Laura had enrolled in strictly academic offerings. It was mentioned earlier that we learn through contrast, and Alissa and Laura provided for me, since by the end of their freshman year, they were on clearly different paths that would lead them to clearly different destinations.

Our art teacher has always excelled at placing student work on display, and I remember well the first time I saw one of Alissa's creations in a showcase by the library. On exhibit were a group of small animals that had been crafted through the use of a variety of left-over, discarded or useless objects. Alissa's caught my eye as she had created what looked like a gleeful and mischievous mouse. Using an old spool of thread, some pipe cleaners, scraps of felt, a burned-out light bulb and other assorted objects, she had developed this adorable object which she had entitled, "Alissa's Mouseterpiece". Perhaps because I have an affinity for collecting ceramic and wooden mice, it was one of the objects on display that regularly caught my eye and I made it a point to seek her out to tell her how much I liked what she had made.

"I love that class," said Alissa, as I offered her my compliments on her work. "I've always done stuff like that." She laughed gaily. "I think it used to drive my mom nuts, 'cause I was always bugging her to take me to the arts and crafts store for something to make. When I was little, there'd be glue, or Play-dough, or paint all over the desk in my room, but my mom still gave me the stuff to play with. I guess it kind of stuck with me, but at least now I get to mess up the art room." She laughed again and moved down the hall towards her next class.

I remember that conversation well simply because I was struck by what a happy child Alissa seemed to be. When I watched her perform with the choir later that semester, I was again caught by how joyous she seemed as she participated in the singing of a variety of holiday standards. She just radiated contentment.

Laura didn't radiate the same joy or happiness. My first opportunity to talk with her came about shortly following the first marking period of her freshman year. Because I was beginning to look at which students would be participating in our summer camp program, I was going through a computer print-out which listed those students who had failed three or more courses during that grading session and Laura's name appeared on the list, having failed five of the six classes she was taking. I brought her to my office to see what could be done to help her find more success in the coming marking period.

"High school is a lot harder than junior high," Laura told me in response to my question as to why she thought she was having a hard time in school. "I don't think I'm smart enough to do some of the things that the teachers ask me to do, and most of it's boring or stupid anyway. But," she said, "my mom and dad are going to send me to a tutor this marking period, so maybe that will help."

After Laura left my office, I pulled her cumulative file to see if her belief that she was "not smart enough" had any validity. In looking through a variety of standardized test scores and measurements, it was clear that, through she was not a genius, she had enough ability to succeed in school, and though she might have to work harder than some students, it was well within her capacity to pass the courses she in which she was enrolled. I hoped that she and her parents were correct that a tutor would be beneficial to her and her learning.

By the end of their ninth grade year, the differences between Alissa and Laura were more marked than they had been when they entered in September. Alissa had passed all of her classes, and though her grades were not exceptionally high, all were at or above a B-minus. She was becoming active in the school, moving out of the typical freshman shyness and getting involved with extra-curricular activities. Laura, on the other hand, was still struggling. Withdrawn and uninvolved in extra-curriculars, due in part perhaps to the after-school tutoring, she was finding little success. Though work with the tutor had offered some benefits, she had still failed four classes in English, math, social studies and physical science.

As their sophomore year began, Alissa's schedule was one that included traditional 10th grade courses, as well as a continuation in choir and enrollment in Art I. Laura's schedule, at parent request, was almost a carbon copy of what it had been the year before. Included were re-takes of the four courses she had failed, right down to having the same teachers for these classes again, with her final two courses being the next level of English and math. The paths that the two girls were traveling began to diverge even more.

It was in the beginning of that second year of high school that Laura began to make her way to my office with greater regularity than she had before. Whereas during the previous year she had only been called to my office to discuss her academic difficulties, by late September, I had seen her on four separate occasions, once for skipping school, once for disrespect towards a teacher, and most disturbing of all, twice for fighting. Her grades were already poor, teachers were reporting that she was failing to turn in assignments or to even attempt the work assigned and that behavioral problems were disrupting the classroom.

In late October of that year, I was in my office with a student

137

who was interviewing me for the school newspaper when we were disrupted by a loud commotion in the outer office. I went out to see Alissa, sobbing and holding a wet paper towel to her cheek. Behind her came a teacher, virtually dragging an angrily screaming Laura towards my office.

"I don't know what happened, exactly," said the teacher, sounding out of breath. "We were working on story maps and I turned towards the board and the next thing I knew, there was shouting and over-turned desks and Laura was over Alissa, yanking at her hair." She shook her head in disbelief. "I ran to break it up, but as I pulled Laura away, she reached out and clawed Alissa's face. I don't have a clue to what started it."

I sent the journalism student out of my office and motioned Alissa into my office. Laura was placed in a conference room around the corner, and the principal went in to talk to her in an effort to calm her down.

I gave Alissa some time to quiet the sobs and then asked her to let me see her cheek. She pulled away the paper towel, revealing three gouges extending from just under her right eye down to the chin.

"I was just sitting there in class," Alissa began when she was able to tell me what had happened. "Ms. Pierce had started to do the story map on the board, and I looked over at Jamie, one of my friends, and reminded her we had an extra choir rehearsal tonight after school." She gulped back another sob. "When I turned back, I looked over at Laura and she said, 'What are you looking at?' so I said, 'Nothing'. The next thing I knew, she was calling me names and telling me to stop looking at her." She continued. "So I told her, 'No problem'. Jamie looked at me and smiled and I guess I kind of shrugged my shoulders. All of a sudden, there was Laura with her hands in my hair, screaming at me. I didn't know what to do." Alissa started to cry again. "I felt so stupid. The whole class was looking at us, and it hurt so bad, I just started crying. Ms. Pierce got over there quickly and yelled at Laura, trying to get her to stop, but as she pulled her away, she reached out and scratched my face." She rubbed the top of her head. "I think she pulled out a bunch of my hair. And I still don't know what I did."

I offered Alissa the phone then to call her mom or dad in case she wanted to go home, and told her I would talk to either of them when they came in to get her. As she picked up the phone, I left my office to talk to Laura.

The principal was coming from the conference room as I came out. He shut the door behind him, but through the window I could see that Laura, though no longer yelling or swearing, was still visibly angry.

"I don't know what the other girl had to say," he said, "But Laura pretty much identified that this was all her fault. She says she's sick of what a 'goodie-goodie' the other gal is and just decided to let her have it." He shook his head. "You can talk to her, but it sure seems pretty cut and dried."

I nodded and went in to talk with Laura. "What? Are you going to kick me out of school now?" she asked with anger. "I'm sick of this fuckin' school anyway, so just kick me out. Then you can keep all your goodie-goodies like Alissa. Those are the only people anyone wants around here anyway."

"In answer to your question, Laura, yes. It would appear that you'll be removed from school for a period of time," I said. "I won't lie to you. But I need to be sure that I have the story straight. Is it true that Alissa had done nothing to you--she hadn't said anything or done anything to cause you to be so angry?"

"She looked at me." Laura said, and noting my look of bewilderment, continued. "I'm just sick of her and people like her. They think they're so great and so wonderful. 'Don't forget choir practice tonight.'" Laura mimicked. "I'm just sick of hearing it and watching how everybody around here treats 'em like they're special. I just decided to show her she wasn't all that great."

"And attacking her was the way to do that?" I asked.

"I'll bet she doesn't think she's so great now." she said smugly.

Laura was suspended for a 10-day period for unprovoked assault and never returned to school. Her parents enrolled her in a local alternative education program the following semester, believing that perhaps she would have greater success there. Alissa returned to school the following day, the marks on her face still in evidence but no other apparent scarring resulted from the experience. She continued to do well in school, passed her classes and upon graduation, enrolled in a college that specialized in art and design.

I'm not sure that I'd have ever fully recognized the contrast between Alissa and Laura had that incident not occurred. Prior to that time, there was nothing that was truly remarkable about them as compared to similar types of students, whether those who do well or those who struggle. But the viciousness with which Laura had attacked, both verbally and physically, left me searching for clues as to how the incident had come about and why she ended up as such an unhappy and lost soul.

In looking through cumulative files on both students, tracking their progress through school from the earliest grades, there was no glaring discrepancies between the skill levels or progress made through school. Movement through the elementaries and junior high level had been unremarkable. Family histories, too, were similar, with both girls coming from intact families and middle class homes. There was, in fact, only one thing that seemed to stand out as I moved through the files and reviewed the past histories: Alissa's records from junior high through high school tracked her enrollment in either an art class or a choir class each semester. Laura's record showed no such enrollment, the closest being her enrollment in a sewing class at the junior high level and as noted, she had enrolled in nothing artistic or creative during her short time at our high school.

Following this observation, I spent a great deal of time reviewing the records of those students who were struggling and failing within the school setting. Almost without exception, I found myself looking at report cards, schedules and cumulative files that were absent any indicators of creative, artistic types of course work. As I went through the records, it also became more and more clear that the files that I was digging through belonged, in large part, not only to students who were failing, but who also were regularly creating disruptions, havoc and problems for themselves and for others both in and out of the school setting.

Laura was only one sad example of this. Unlike Alissa whose parents had obviously provided her with avenues for creative outlets from the earliest age, Laura had not had the same opportunities. It would be ridiculous to suggest that her parents were guilty of neglect for not assuring her the opportunities to develop her creative potential; it is more a part of the world we live in where fewer and fewer people recognize the inherent value in having time to exercise our need to create. Having been raised and moving through the schools from the late 1950's on, during the time of increasing emphasis on science, math and technology, Laura's parents, like millions of other parents, were undoubtedly educated that intellectual skills were the ones that needed to be cultivated through the schools and the society. Areas of intuitive, creative growth were relegated to the optional--areas that would be nurtured only as an afterthought. In some homes, like Alissa's, this happened. Sadly, in too many others, it did not.

It was noted earlier that the need to create is not one that will be set aside, and if the value of positive creativity is not taught, nurtured and exercised, a very different form of creativity emerges. Laura exemplified this. Lacking the skills, knowledge, or wherewithal to produce and create in a positive manner, she was left to create in ways destructive to others and to herself. Not only was she unable to create positively, the other soul needs so intertwined with creativity--self-reliance, love, belonging and simplicity were absent as well. She had never learned how to pull something out of her own heart and soul and put it onto paper for the world to see. She had missed out on the opportunities to have her creativity recognized and applauded by significant people in her life. She was without the opportunities to work with others in the production of an artistic endeavor. And as she struggled in school and found herself repeating course work, her movement through the educational system became less simple, more complex and more restricted.

We all need to create. It is an essential nutrient for the soul, and when creativity is allowed to grow and flourish, it offers growth and development of the other soul needs as well. Yet as we look at the world around us, it often seems that there are fewer and fewer people that recognize and understand the value of positive creativity, and seek instead to exercise this need through the negative creations such as self-defeating dramas and hardships, graffiti, violence and destruction. This is easily identified, not only in the society at large but in the schools as well, and as the schools seek to do the best they can do to truly educate the "whole child", they need to recognize that encouraging the development of their students' creative potential is an integral part of the schools' mission.

CREATIVITY IN THE SCHOOLS

As questions abound in our society as to whether we are "dumbing down" our curriculum in American schools, and as policy makers regularly wring their hands over declining test scores and American students' poor showing against their foreign counterparts, the recognition of the value of course work in the creative areas is rapidly being dismissed as less important than emphasis in the intellectual realm. Yet as this is dismissed, so too is any semblance of balance that can be provided for our children. As students leave our high schools through graduation, dropping out or dismissal, more of them are leaving without a balance between the intellect and the soul and are moving into a world where they are creating in negative ways to the detriment of themselves and those around them. While it may be difficult for educational policy makers to defend the value of arts-related course work in light of the demands for intellectual and work place skills coming from all sides, those who recognize the value of the souls of our students will find themselves more willing to defend the return and inclusion of such courses in the lives of our students.

Like those soul needs previously mentioned, the opportunities to develop in creative areas was once an integral part of the public school curriculum. Children in the elementary grades were given the opportunity for art and music, for coloring and singing, for story creation and imaginary play. At the secondary level, elective opportunities were once more plentiful and accessible than they are at present, and students had various options to enroll in course work that would meet such needs, even if they did not involve themselves in those extra-curricular options that fell within the creative realm. Likewise, within the homes of America, children were once more apt to involve themselves in creative play and activities and to have such play recognized and nurtured by the parents within the home. But with those rapid technological advances being made following Sputnik; with the growth of the media and television to provide entertainment for children and adults; with video games and computers within homes to occupy time, the inherent ability and desire to entertain oneself through creative play and activities slowly lost ground. Within homes, children were less likely to color and draw and create imaginative games since the television was there to provide entertainment for them. Since greater numbers of families had two parents working outside the home, less guidance was available to children to keep them from depending on the television or video games for entertainment. As their reliance on this outside medium grew, their ability to tap into the creative potential of their souls declined.

Within the schools, this trend was mirrored. Those technological advances and strides being made modified what was needed by people who were to be productive and efficient members in the world of work. Schools were pushed, prodded, and demanded to increase standards, to teach science, math and technology, to prepare their students for the world they would enter. The resulting consequence was that as curricular demands in these areas increased, the curricular availabilities in the course work that involved creativity, introspection and aesthetics decreased. Typically, for those students who came from homes where a recognition and appreciation for arts and creativity remained, this movement had less impact and though they had fewer options to exercise this soul need during the regular school day, they were still available to them through the home and through the extra-curriculars in which they were more likely to get involved. For those students whose homes did not place a strong emphasis on the creative needs of children, the diminishing opportunities for creative outlet had more profound impact. The six to seven hour school day for these children could conceivably consist of only a strict academic schedule and for many of them, there was little to look forward to during an average school day. Those who were doing passably well or better found themselves and their time taken up by the studying, reports and tests that naturally came with their classes. There just wasn't the time to get involved with extra-curriculars where they might find enjoyment through the simple and creative. For those who struggled, their dislike of the school grew as they failed classes and got caught up in that vicious circle of having to repeat those required for the diploma. These, too, were not likely to involve themselves in the extra-curricular areas. For them, such opportunities represented nothing more than additional time spent in a school setting where they were unhappy and disconnected.

The correlation between the educational trend towards the intellectual and logical over the past few decades and the increase in behavioral problems being seen among American youth both within and outside of the schools is one that should be closely examined. Our students will create, and as noted, what we need to look at is whether they will create in positive or negative ways. For the students who are involved in music, theater, fine arts, and even athletics, they are finding ways to create that nurture and exercise their souls. For the other students who have not developed the means for positive creation, both those within and those outside of the schools find them creating in negative ways and these impact both them and those around them. To return to a balance between the intellectual and creative is to not only serve these students, but also to serve the rest of the school population and, indirectly, the society as well. Again, this can be easily accomplished with virtually no expense or restructuring, but simply an altered focus as to what it is that our children need to be whole and balanced.

Within the elementary schools of America there needs to be a renewed recognition of that value of childhood mentioned previously. Childhood is that time where the creative needs and urges are still intact and are an inherent part of life. Educators again need to work to assess whether the changes they make in the curriculum of their elementary schools will serve to damage or diminish the time available for their students to be involved in creative play, art, music and story-telling. With any new innovation, trend or demand that shortens the time available to children for creativity, the foundations of their souls are slowly chipped away. As mentioned, for some of the students, depending upon home situations, this will have lesser impact. For others, as their outlets for creativity through the schools are lost, they will become unhappier and will experience greater dissatisfaction with their schooling. Not only will they weaken their natural ability and need to create in positive ways, they will begin the movement to create the negative and will therefore begin the establishment of that vicious circle that they may end up powerless to break.

So as to preclude this, elementary schools must maintain a constant recognition as to the value of creativity. Children must be allowed the time and the opportunities to engage in art, music, drama, and creative writing, not only during after-school times, but during the regular school day so that those who are not likely to remain after school for such opportunities still have access to them. Student work in the creative realm needs to receive as much recognition and appreciation and approval as does their work in the intellectual areas, so as to enhance its continuation. Demands from business and industry to emphasize work-related learning and skills at the elementary level should be seen for what it is: developmentally inappropriate for the students at the lower grade levels. Surely they can be exposed to career days and similar activities, but not at the expense of their time for creative work. Schools can work towards improved standardized test scores, but not to the exclusion of creative and artistic experiences. Each teacher within the elementary schools across our country can set aside a portion of every school day to allow students time to write poetry, to paint, to draw, to work with clay, or any other activity that will allow not only for the exercise of the creative needs of the soul, but also which will enhance their self-reliance, their sense of love and belonging and their access to the simple in life. Each teacher can balance out the school day between the needs for the intellect and the needs of the soul.

The secondary schools of America are no different in this, though as students move closer and closer to graduation, their movement through the schools is marked by an increased need and demand to exit the public schools with the skills and abilities to be productive and efficient, whether moving directly into the work force or into a college or trade school. They are different as well in that the behavioral and academic difficulties demonstrated by growing numbers of students enrolled in our secondary schools are often more observable and serious than those found in the elementary schools. This should not come as any big surprise, since, as noted earlier, by the time a child has moved into the secondary school level, they have invariably either established a connection with the school or are disconnected from it. It is those who are not connected with the school in a positive way that bring in a host of problems in the form of negative creations that school personnel are regularly forced to address.

Positive creativity can easily be incorporated, expanded, emphasized and maintained in any secondary school without any major changes or expenditures. It simply requires that those responsible for guiding and scheduling students into the appropriate academic path recognize that all students, regardless of intelligence, ability, career goals or post-high school plans, will benefit from the opportunity to develop in the creative areas. With such recognition, the adults who work with students will be more likely to encourage and even require some type of creative outlet during the school day. Since such opportunities can be so plentiful and so readily available, the first requirement for the adults within the school is to see to it that all students make use of these opportunities.

Laura was typical of a student who did not access such opportunities and whose parents did not see the importance of advocating her involvement in the creative areas. This is not atypical for many students currently enrolled in our high schools for that previously mentioned reason that there just is not a great deal of value placed on creativity in the world today. Students who are advanced-placed or above average are encouraged to enroll in a demanding schedule of academic course work so that they can be better prepared for college. Students who tread the middle of the road, likewise, are encouraged into a solid core of academics so that they can be best prepared for moving into a trade or technical school, or directly into the world of work. Those students who are struggling, as noted, are busy attempting to catch up with classes that they have failed in the past and are regularly counseled into repeating failed courses and too often miss out on the opportunities to enroll in the creative.

Yet for any of these, the inclusion of a class or an extra-curricular activity where there is the opportunity to exercise and strengthen the soul's need for creativity allows for some balance that will enable the student to function more happily. Rather than pushing the high achievers or average students into strictly academic schedules, the adults who guide these students in the schools can see to it that each child's schedule has some outlet for creative expression, whether through creative writing, art, music, or theater. Rather than dismissing the arts as optional activities, each student enrolled can be encouraged or even required to enroll in one such course during each semester of their school career. To do so ensures that at some point during each school day the student will have access to all of the benefits involved in positive creation.

For the lower achieving student, the same is true, yet there is one additional point that should be brought in here. Across the country, industrial arts, woodworking, auto shop, and other similar classes are finding themselves in peril within the schools. More and more, these types of courses are seen as either "outmoded", or better left within vocational or technical centers. Yet for many struggling students, such classes are their preferred mode of positive creation and as these classes are weeded out of the public schools, also being weeded out are the few remaining places that the average or struggling students often chose so as to find enjoyment, positive creativity and success. These have often been a safe haven for these students who needed to create but who felt out of place in the theater, art or music room. When these classes are eliminated from the curricular offerings of a school, it serves to send a very strong message to such students that their wants, needs and desires are of little importance in the world of academics. These students are less likely to connect with the school anyway and to send such a message often cements their belief that the school cares little for them. This engenders anger among the students and, particularly since there are now fewer classes available where they can exercise creativity in a positive way, their creations tend to move down more negative pathways.

This being the case, again it is in the best interest of not only such students but also the school to see classes in woodworking, industrial arts, or auto shop not as relics of the past, but as very necessary components in the school day of a sizable number of students. In maintaining such opportunities the school not only sends the message that in recognizes the needs and wants of the students who enroll, but it also guarantees a creative outlet for these children who need one as much as do the other students within the school.

The world at large will continue to work at eradicating childhood and dismissing the creativity that is such an inherent and essential part. This is only a sad fact of the increasingly technological, complex and hectic society that we live in. Yet schools need to be a defender of childhood and to hold tightly to the realization that we do a disservice to our children if we eliminate their opportunities for creative pursuits. We need to recognize that within American homes, fewer children are finding guidance towards positive creativity and if they do not learn how to create things of goodness and beauty, they will create things that are negative and destructive. This being the case and factoring in the further understanding that the schools are the one place where we are assured that virtually all children will attend at one time or another, it only makes sense for us to exercise, stretch and nurture the souls of our students by providing them with the means to become creative and creating beings.

CHAPTER 7

Nature as a Need of the Soul

There is an old adage which states that "what goes around, comes around" and this is, in fact, one of the sayings that we incorporate as a theme in our yearly U-Turn camp with our high potential-low achieving students. It is one of those concepts that seems important for them as well as the rest of us to understand since all of life does follow a circular pattern. For our students, in using this as a theme for our program, it has been our hope and our belief that they can come to understand that in the cyclical process of life, the circles set up can be either functional or dysfunctional and, with the proper knowledge and understanding they can better set up functional circles in their lives and break out of the dysfunctional ones in which they are so trapped. In working with our students in a camp setting, we are within an environment that provides ready access to and demonstration of all the lessons that our natural world has to offer. These lessons from nature are important ones for our children and our students since they reveal a natural flow and illustrate how to best blend into the world around us in a functional way.

Yet as our society has moved from an agrarian society to the industrial age and into the information age, we have also moved away from the lessons that nature has to offer, including lessons in self-sufficiency and self-reliance, in the wisdom of simplicity and in the joy of beauty. In so distancing ourselves and our young people from these lessons, we are also further removed from the cyclical process that is found in nature and as a result, distanced as well from the soul.

NATURAL STRENGTH FOR THE SOUL

The value of nature and all that it has to offer us in terms of strengthening the soul has indeed been lost over the past decades as we have created an increasingly industrial, informational and complex world. As society has evolved, it has increased its reliance on the logical, technological and the complex. The resultant decrease has been seen in those things that are intuitive, natural and simple and while there is a fairly substantial resurgence in the recognition that we need to care for our natural world and environment, there is lesser focus on the realization that it is through the lessons of that world and environment that we can exercise and strengthen our own souls and the souls of our children and students as well. Through nature not only are valuable lessons available, but we also can access the previously mentioned soul-needs as well, in ways not generally available in the hectic, day-to-day complexity in which we find ourselves.

In a world where we are constantly bombarded by a deluge of outside voices sending us information that we need to process, there is little time and fewer and fewer places where we can find access to peace and solitude and have the quiet to hear those inner voices and the wisdom there offered. Without taking the time for this, our ability to practice self-reliance and self-trust is diminished and our reliance on those outside voices is intensified. Through time to walk in natural settings, away from the hustle of day to day life and away from the noise of those outside voices, our ability to tap into the wisdom of the inner voice is enhanced. Along with this, in taking the time to move away from the complexity of the world around us and into the simplicity of nature, we are freed, if only temporarily, from the pressures of day to day life and the complexity with which we constantly find life cluttered. When you tie in the understanding that in removing ourselves from this complexity, it is also easier to tap into our creative potential through the natural beauty found around us, it becomes even more clear why time spent in the simplicity of nature is so valuable to the soul.

For ourselves as well as our children, nature also directly teaches lessons necessary to the development of the soul. These lessons include the way in which nature cares for itself in a functional circle of life if it is left undisturbed by human influence and that it is only when the natural flow is disrupted that dysfunction results. Through observing nature, lessons in non-resistance and self-reliance are taught that are applicable to our own day to day lives. And perhaps most important for our children who live in a world which doesn't often teach this lesson, through the wisdom of nature it can be learned that what goes around truly does come around and, if left undisturbed by human intervention or influence, all things do turn out for the best.

In stopping to consider where these lessons are taught in the world at present or how often any of us have the time to simply immerse ourselves in natural settings away from the hurried pace of our lives, it is clear that there are few if any places where such lessons are found. Likewise, the flow of most of our lives at present is one that precludes us from regularly moving from the complexity of our world to the simplicity of nature. Yet as this has become less likely, we have increasingly sent a message to our children that such things are not valuable and have lessened their access and their time to enjoy nature and learn its lessons; enjoyment and lessons that would provide for nurture and strength to their souls.

153

A STUDY IN CONTRAST: ALAN AND JOHN

There is something to be said for working in a smaller school within a community that is comprised of both rural and more urban settings, particularly if you are learning through the contrast between the children raised in either setting and their view of life in the world around them. As I looked at the soul-strengthening benefits found in nature and in understanding natural flow, I was also seeing the difference between the soulfulness of the children raised in a rural setting, perhaps on a farm, where natural flow was part and parcel, and those raised in a more urban setting where access to nature was not an inherent part of life. Alan and John were such a study in contrast and provided me with greater understanding and recognition of the importance of nature and natural flow to the soul.

Alan and John were both juniors in high school the year that I got to know the two of them. They were good friends, but it seemed an unlikely pairing. John was tall and thin, with pale blonde hair and penetrating blue eyes, where Alan was short and stocky, with dark brown hair and big brown eyes. Apart from these surface differences, they were unlike in other respects as well. John came from an intact family, who for the past three generations had operated a mid-sized dairy farm south of town. A quiet young man, his life away from school consisted largely of getting up before dawn to complete farm chores, moving through his school day, including football practices in the fall and basketball practices in the winter, and then returning home to more farm duties and his homework. To the average teenager who knew little of such a life, John's daily routine seemed a difficult and unrewarding one, overall. His schedule limited his time and opportunity to participate in the other activities in which his peers were regularly involved. He missed

154

school dances, avoided the parties that were weekend fixtures, and spent little time at the local mall, a favorite pastime for many of his classmates.

John's friend, on the other hand, missed no such opportunities. Outgoing and social, Alan was a regular fixture at dances and parties. He held down a part-time job in a sporting goods store at the mall, and when not working, could often be seen simply "hanging out" in the mall's food court or video arcade. He spent little time at home, perhaps due to the fact that there was never anyone else there. His parents had split up when he was twelve, and his mother worked second shift as a nurse, leaving home before school was out, and returning after he was asleep. Alan, too, participated in football and basketball, and it was through these activities that he and John had become friends; they had little else in common.

I had not known either John or Alan well prior to their junior year in high school since neither of them ever demonstrated any problems with attendance or discipline, the two primary means through which I got to know students. At the beginning of their junior year they had signed up to be office assistants during their third hour class period. Assistant positions were available to those students who were on track for graduation and who had some flexibility in their schedule. During the semester, it was their job to collect the hourly attendance sheets, run errands or complete other tasks assigned to them. Because the duties were not terribly taxing, there was often time for the assistants to study, or assist teachers if needed, or to simply take some time to chat with the secretaries, counselors or administrators in the office. For me, when time permitted, it was always nice to have the opportunity to talk with students about other things of interest to them, without having to discuss issues of discipline and attendance and over the course of that first semester of their junior year, I had a number of chances to sit and talk with Alan and John about school, sports, their hobbies, their girlfriends and their future plans.

I'm not sure that I would have ever fully recognized the marked differences between these two young men had it not been for one day, shortly before the holiday recess, that I noticed that Alan seemed withdrawn and subdued, a definite contrast from his normal, gregarious character. He'd been sitting at a table near the counter, either looking at a paper in front of him or alternately lying his head down. Having left my office to get a file, I moved past him, touched him on the shoulder and questioned whether he was feeling alright or if he was ill. He assured me gruffly that he was fine, so I left him be and continued with my work. A short time later, I noticed that John had returned to the office with the hourly attendance which he had collected on his own, though it was a job that he and Alan usually completed together. I called him into my office.

"Is there a problem with Alan?" I asked him. "If he's sick and needs to go home, I can get a hold of his mom. Or is there something else wrong."

John smiled. "He's okay, Mrs. Lawrence," he assured me. "I think he's just frustrated. He hardly got any playing time in the game last night--got pulled after just a minute and a half, after he missed his first two shots. Then he and his girlfriend got into a fight and today, she sent him some letter that's got him all upset." He looked thoughtful then. "I'm just leaving him be and letting him work through it--though I did tell him when it rains, it pours, but I don't think he appreciated that very much--hasn't talked to me since. So I'm just leaving him be. When he's ready, he'll talk if he wants to. He always does."

I once heard a student who was speaking at a conference remark that there was a "fine line between adults being there and being in the way" and it was a comment that I have always remembered, so I took John's words regarding Alan to heart and chose to leave him alone and not be "in the way". I assumed that, as his friend had noted, when the time was right for him he would either move past his frustration or find someone to talk with.

The next morning, Alan stopped me in the hallway. "Would you have a few minutes to talk with me today?" he asked. He looked much the same as yesterday, and his voice was quiet and subdued. I told him that I'd have time as soon as first hour classes got underway and asked if he'd like me to send for him then.

"I can't miss my math class first hour," he said. "We have a test and I'm already behind on a couple of assignments. And second hour I have to do a speech. So if its okay with you, maybe we could just talk for a little bit during third hour, when I'm in the office anyway." I told him that would be fine and he headed off down the hall towards his first hour class.

When third hour rolled around, Alan appeared at my office door. "Do you have time now, Mrs. L.?" he asked. I motioned him into my office and he sat down in the chair next to my desk.

"So what's up, Alan?" I asked. "You haven't seemed yourself and I didn't want to pry yesterday."

"I really just want your opinion," he said. "I'm thinking of quitting the basketball team, but I don't want to hurt my chances of playing a spring sport and I don't want the football coach to think badly of me come next fall during football tryouts. I just wondered if there are any rules or anything that could keep me from playing baseball or running track in the spring if I decide to."

Taking the question at face value, I looked up athletic rules in the school handbook and verified for Alan that there were no rules that would preclude him from participation in another sport during the next season should he choose to quit playing basketball. Having assured him of that, I asked why he was thinking of quitting.

"I just hate it," he said. "I don't like it. I'm not all that good at it and the coach doesn't let me play long enough during a game to even get warmed up. It'll show him if I quit. He just can't play all his favorites and expect the rest of us to just sit the bench and wait 'til we're up by 20 points to play for a couple minutes." He paused for a moment. "What do you think I should do?" he asked.

I thought for a second before I answered. "I think you should do what you think is best, not what I think. But I do suggest that you reconsider quitting if it's just in an effort to 'show the coach' or to teach him something. Your leaving the team may not have that effect at all."

Alan laughed briefly. "You're right about that," he said. "He might not even miss me...but the other players would miss how well I warm the bench." He grew more serious then. "I just get so frustrated. It seems like I work so hard, and I try to do the right things and it just doesn't help. In fact, the more frustrated I get, the worse it seems to go. Kinda like with Pam too."

"I thought maybe there were some problems with your girlfriend," I told him. "You were pouring over that letter yesterday for most of the hour. Are things not going well there?"

"It's the same thing as the basketball," Alan responded. "I try to do all the right things--take her where she wants to go, eat lunch with her instead of my friends, walk her to class, even if it makes me tardy. But I still end up doing something she doesn't like, and then she's mad and I'm mad, and then the rest of the day seems to just get all screwed up." He clenched his fists in frustration. "I just feel like the harder I work at everything these days, the worse it gets. I'm not making anything better, I'm just making everything worse."

At that point, John appeared at the office door to tell me I had a phone call. I excused myself and turned to the phone, noting as I did that John had plunked himself down in the chair next to the door. While I took the phone call, he and Alan talked quietly. When I had finished, I turned back to the two students, now deeply engrossed in their conversation.

"It's like when we have a problem on the farm, with the crops or the weather or the animals," John was saying. "We don't fight against what's happening. We have to work with it...or we don't just get frustrated--we end up losing time or money or an animal. So my dad taught me early on to take what nature offers you and then work with it--not against it." He laughed. "I'm pretty sure that my dad knew that I could apply that other places too, like here at school." John looked at me then. "I'm sorry that I just barged in. Alan was telling me about wanting to quit the basketball team and I was just telling some of my dad's farm wisdom."

"What I heard made sense to me," I told him. "But what about you, Alan? You two can use my office for awhile if you want to just talk this through. John may have more sound advice to offer than I have."

"That's okay, Mrs. L.," Alan said. "I don't think all that stuff about the farm really applies much to what I'm dealing with here." He rubbed at the arm of the chair with his fist, looking discouraged. "I'm talking about coaches and girlfriends and problems with people, not animals or crops or the weather. It's just not the same thing." He looked over at John. "I know you're trying to help, but you just don't understand what I'm talking about."

John nodded. "That's what I always told my dad when I got mad about something at school or with a friend or coach. I'd be

159

all set to fight whatever it was and my dad would just nod and say, 'Go ahead, but remember that the tree that doesn't bend when the strong wind comes up is not a tree that survives the storm. If you want to fight against it, it's your call, but if you want to be a survivor, you'll learn how to work with it.' A few times fighting situations that shouldn't have been fought were enough to bring those words right back into my head." He looked over at me. "I don't get frustrated much anymore, though I remember when I was a freshman a few times I really felt like I was beating my head against a wall, trying to change something that couldn't be changed. After awhile, I got tired of beating myself up and I started to listen to what my dad said."

Alan was starting to fidget. "Yeah? Well, I am going to quit the team and I will tell the coach a thing or two when I do." He stood up and moved towards the door. "And the same for Pam. She'll be sorry for how she treated me when I tell her we're not going to go out anymore." He turned and walked out of my office and seconds later I heard the door to the main office swing shut behind him. John just shook his head.

"As long as I've known Alan he's seemed to have a short fuse," he said. "He gets frustrated for awhile and eventually gets past it, but usually not until he's made things worse and has had to go back and correct things." He stood up to leave my office. "He's a good friend though, and I wish I could help him more than I do, but, like my dad says, 'A tree that's going to survive doesn't fight the strong wind, and sometimes Alan's like a very strong wind, and I either bend or just stay out of the way."

It took me some time after that conversation with and between these two students to come to an understanding of how and why they were so different in their attitudes and their approach towards life. Apart from the fact that one came from an intact family and the other from a single-parent home, there was little that could account for the different outlooks. I mentioned this to a colleague, pondering aloud the differences between these two.

"You'll almost always see that kind of an attitude among those children who've been raised on a farm," he commented. "They grow up learning about nature and the natural flow of the world around them. They live with life and death and the circle of nature and life on a daily basis and it becomes ingrained in their being." He went on with his explanation. "For other students who haven't had the same experiences, they've lived with the flow of life being what they see in the artificial world around them, on television, at movies, in their homes. They've been taught that human's can control everything, and so they think that they can. The frustration comes in when they realize that not only are some things outside their power to control, but that some things you shouldn't try to control." He continued with a wry grin.

"I have a friend who married into the farm life. As she was driving by one of the local farms a few weeks back, and she noticed that there was a cow giving birth out in the field. She knew enough to tell that the cow seemed to be having trouble and that there was no one around. She pulled her car into the driveway of the house and went up to the door to inform the family that they needed to get some help out to this cow." He smiled again. "A young girl, one of our students, in fact, came to the door. 'Can I help you?' she asked, to which this friend of mine answered that there was a cow in the field giving birth and seemingly was in need of help. 'Thanks', the girl told her. 'We know about it, though, and we know she's having trouble.'

" 'Shouldn't you get a vet out to help?' asked my friend, to which the girl quite calmly answered no. 'The veterinarian's bill would be more than the calf is worth,' she'd said, 'So we're just letting nature take the course that it will.'"

I looked at him, horrified, as he finished the story. "That's the same look she had on her face when she told me about it," he said. "But what you and she don't understand is that people who grow up and are raised on a farm or anywhere else where they learn the lessons that nature has to teach, recognize that there is a purpose and a function to everything that happens. They believe and live by the philosophy that what goes around comes around and that there is a natural process to all things that should not be circumvented or controlled."

"That was the difference between the two students today," he continued. "One wanted to control the people that he saw as standing in the way of what he wanted and the other recognized that to all things there is a natural flow that you either work with or get broken down and frustrated with in working against it."

I reflected on the learning I had just gained and considered the two students again. Alan would seemingly move through life, seeking to control things to his advantage, meeting frustration and anger when it didn't go as planned. John, on the other hand, would most likely take those things that life had to offer and work with them to the best of his ability, meeting little frustration and believing fully that all things would work out for the best overall. It was an interesting contrast and a memorable lesson.

The learning gained from Alan and John did more than just verify the value found in the lessons of the natural world around us. For me, it also helped to solidify an understanding that along with the self-reliance, simplicity, beauty and creativity that are so necessary to the full development of the soul, so too is an understanding and appreciation of nature. In coming to such understanding, one develops the wisdom that all things work out for the best and that to seek control over the natural process of things is to create dysfunction and frustration and along with this wisdom comes a tie-in to all the other soul needs as well.

Through learning that natural flow is not something that can be circumvented or controlled, we are less likely to be swayed by those outside voices that promise that they can assist us in controlling the things that are happening in our lives. We are less likely to believe advertisers' claims that one product or another can bring us health, wealth and happiness, for a price. We are not as swayed by the advice of others who suggest that we fudge on our income taxes or cheat on a test. We are not likely to attempt controlling others through violence or aggression. We become more at peace and more self-reliant.

Likewise, through the lessons and appreciation of nature, we can come to recognize how simple things can be and how well they can turn out if they are left undisturbed and unimpeded and how disastrous things can be when we seek to exert our influence and control. In my neighborhood, for years the residents sought to establish country-club caliber lawns, pouring fertilizer and nutrients on their yards to create their definition of beauty. Their complicated lawn care had a side-effect, however, as the fertilizers and nutrients washed down a hill, towards a little lake a few thousand yards away. Where it was once a small lake, it is now a tiny one, overgrown with vegetation and without enough oxygen to support the fish that once inhabited it, a sad testimony to the consequences of humans' disrupting the natural flow of an area.

The beauty of our natural world is, as well, essential to the soul. There are few people that will not stand in awe at the splendor of the Rocky Mountains in the distance; who will not relish the glory of the sunrise over the Atlantic; who don't smile at the appearance of a rainbow in the sky after a rain. The

163

beauty and quiet of a morning walk through a quiet wood or forest, the glimmer of the sun reflecting off freshly fallen snow, or any other of nature's gifts of beauty are refreshing to the soul and offer us not only beauty, but a sense of peace as well.

And for whatever reasons, taking the time to move into nature and surround ourselves with it allows us greater access to our creative potentials as well. Perhaps because we are not being bombarded by countless other information sources and distractions and perhaps because we are therefore more likely to be able to hear our inner voice, taking time in natural settings enhances our ability to be creative and to think. In many ways, taking the time to appreciate and immerse ourselves in the beauty of nature sets up a functional circle in which our soul is exercised through the beauty and simplicity of the natural world and this in turn opens up the creative potentials of the soul which lead to even greater appreciation of those natural settings. It's a truly valuable circle.

While there is, as noted, a resurgence of interest in our natural world and in taking care of the environment around us, our schools place little value or emphasis upon the lessons to be found in nature as they relate to our day to day lives and surely no mention is made as to the soul benefits there. We may look at the need to protect the forests and the waterways and instill these lessons in our students, but rarely do we use nature to teach the lessons that John had learned so well on the farm--that to all things there is a purpose and a flow and that through nature we can learn how to best operate in the world and with the people around us. But it is through such lessons that our students not only can become more functional participants in the world that they are entering, as well they can gain the soul-strengthening benefits that enable them to become more whole individuals.

THE VALUE OF NATURE:
NOT FOR BIOLOGY CLASSES ONLY

I have always been dismayed by the diminishing amount of natural light found in the vast majority of schools across our country. Whether compact, multi-storied city schools or sprawling one-story suburban or rural buildings, the limited number of windows letting natural light into the schools of America, though a testimony to energy consciousness, can also be seen as symbolic of the ways in which our schools shut out nature's lessons and the balm it can offer to the soul. It seems time now, as the world becomes more complicated and stressful, more violent and ugly, to return the simplicity and beauty of nature to our schools and to allow its help and its lessons in assuring our children the chance to be whole and happy individuals.

In order to best assess how our schools can either return to or move towards including nature in the lives and lessons of their students, it is first essential to look again at the movement of the schools as it is today. In building up the emphasis on technology and work place skills and learning, lesser time and stress has been placed, as previously discussed, on those things that are worthwhile due to their inherent beauty, simplicity and naturalness. Credibility and value has been given to the complicated, the artificial and the structured, not only in the lessons students are required to learn, but also in those things that define success in the world at large.

In looking at the contrasts between the two students, Alan and John, the natural wisdom that John had acquired over his life time seemed the result not only of the lessons that his father had taught him but also those he was more apt to learn simply because his days consisted of regular work outside in natural settings, away from the constant influx of information coming via the television and other media. The most prevalent and influential education he received from his earliest days was that which came via the natural flow of his farm life and the reinforcement of these lessons through his father.

Alan's life, on the other hand, had no such lessons in natural flow. His primary educators throughout his life had been the media and those who had been educated by it. He had grown up believing that there was little in life that could not be controlled or mastered and he met with anger and frustration if his control of a given situation was thwarted. He'd never been taught the value of nature and the lessons to be had there, and as such, continually sought to manage situations in his life through artificial means.

Alan was not unlike many students in our schools today. As we have moved from that agrarian society that once marked us and moved into the industrial and information age, fewer and fewer students have been raised with the lessons of nature once prevalent in our agricultural society and have been raised instead with the lessons of our technological world. We can easily correlate the movement away from the farms with the rising amount of discontent and dysfunction found among the inhabitants of our world and are wise to question how nature's lessons can be incorporated back into the lives of our youth.

Within the schools at present, however, it is the type of education that Alan received that is taught and reinforced. The increasing emphasis on math, science, technology and work-place skills, all logical and linear-sequential, limit the time available for the work that is intuitive and cyclical--much like nature. In neglecting, limiting or dismissing the areas of creativity and beauty and without such lessons from the natural world around them, our students have less access and learning that offers the soul the simplicity, beauty and recognition that "what goes around comes around" and the wisdom that is inherent with this. The resulting consequence is that fewer students are able to operate in other than a complex, structured manner and develop trust that they will always be able to find the means to control the events of their life. When such learning is challenged, frustration and anger and the problems that come with these are invariably the result.

Within elementary schools then, it seems vital that we maintain an understanding and appreciation of the natural world around us and as educators, model this for our students. To do otherwise sends the message to students that there is little value to be had through the wisdom of nature and in these formative years that lesson will be one that sticks. To model a recognition of the value in nature requires little more than maintaining students' access to outside play time and activities. The beauty of the autumn colors; the cold, soft touch of a snowflake on the face; or the greening of the spring foliage provide these, our youngest students, with freedom from the increasingly complex learning that they face on a daily basis. As well, it provides them with enjoyment, pleasure and simplicity that nourishes their soul.

Within the elementary schools, there is already a heavy emphasis on teaching our children concern and care for the environment and so incorporating the lessons that can be had through nature is easily accomplished. Parallels between Mother Nature and human nature abound. Through lessons about recycling students can learn about the circular process that is nature, and that, as with non-recyclable materials, when you disrupt the natural flow of things, harm and dysfunction is the result. Through examining what happens following a forest fire, flood or other natural disaster children can see that even without human intervention, nature will eventually work to reestablish itself. Through lessons from the animal world they can learn that those who are the most self-reliant and self-sufficient are the ones that survive. While there is no great need to offer students these examples as analogies to their own lives, learning for which they are not yet perhaps developmentally ready, it is education that will provide a basis for greater understanding of natural flow as it relates to their own lives later in their educational career.

This brings us to the secondary schools of today. It is important to remember that our students are entering with twelve or thirteen years of education from both in and outside of the schools which vastly impacts the way they see life and much of this education has come via the media which does not readily teach the value of nature or natural flow. For this reason it is not only important to establish for our secondary school students an understanding of the lessons of nature as they relate to their lives but as well maintain for them course work that provides the cyclical, intuitive opportunities that their soul needs.

This first is less easily accomplished than the second, but is still well within the opportunities available in the current system. As in the elementary schools, the lessons being given in science and biology classes lend themselves nicely to drawing parallels between Mother Nature and human nature and at this level, students are more developmentally ready to comprehend the associations there. Like John who recognized that "a tree won't fight a strong wind and survive", our students can likewise come to understand that when they operate by following the laws of nature, they will benefit.

These laws of nature are many and varied and include concepts such as "the survival of the fittest", through which students can see that in both our natural world and in our human society, those who are the most self-reliant are those that survive in the world. Like their elementary counterparts, they can come to understand through lessons about the environment and recycling that disrupting the natural process of the world around us, whether in nature or in human interactions, is to create harm and dysfunction. Through learning about the circle of life and the balance of nature, they can come to understand that when we intervene in this circle, we throw off a balance that is necessary to the well-being of an entire system, which can be related to our desire to control or intervene in all of the events in our lives. Through opportunities to work on projects that take them into wetlands or forests or mountains, they can have the opportunity to soak in the beauty of undisturbed settings. They can learn that, in nature, truly what goes around comes around and that for that reason it is important not to try to hurry, delay or circumvent all of the circumstances of their lives. Through learning about and watching nature and in coming to understand the natural flow of the world around them, they can begin to realize that, in time, all things will and do work out as they should in the great scheme of things, and with this recognition comes an inner peace that nourishes the soul.

In addition to this, schools can, again, maintain those courses which exercise students' inherent, natural desire for beauty and creativity, courses that are intuitive and cyclical. Rather than relegating these to the extra-curricular realm, such course work can be seen as meeting children's need for balance between this and the other classes that are more logical and linear-sequential. It is through such opportunities that students have the chance to travel pathways much like those found in nature--ones that are winding, have no clear destination, and are filled with beauty, simplicity and the need for self-reliance. Once again, since these things are so easily accomplished, have little, if any cost attached to them, and are so beneficial to the souls of children, the question is not a matter of whether we should do them, but whether we can afford not to.

Our souls, and the souls of the children in American schools hunger for the simplicity and beauty found in nature. "To the body and mind which have been cramped by noxious work or company," wrote Emerson. "nature is medicinal and restores their tone."[1] We all often find ourselves in situations that leave us feeling "cramped" or frustrated or confused and surely the same can be said for our children. For this reason and because of the valuable lessons that come as part and parcel with nature, it is one more soul-need that should be included, maintained or restored in American schools.

CHAPTER 8

Faith Within Our Schools

Once upon a time in America, there was such a thing as baccalaureate, a religious ceremony for high school seniors that generally preceded the graduation ceremony. It also was once common practice to include a prayer just prior to school programs and presentations. It used to be that coaches had no fear of a lawsuit if they chose to lead their team in prayer before a game. And here in Michigan, it used to be that a portrait of Jesus Christ hung in the hallway of a public school, causing no controversy and creating hardship for no one. While this may still be America, it certainly isn't once upon that time any more. In this increasingly litigious society, even the thought of offering thanks to the most non-secular God during a school function sends shivers up the spines of school administrators and boards of education. So these days, a short moment of silence is about all the bravest of those in decision-making positions within the schools will allow.

Now for anyone who has undertaken reading this book with a certain degree of comfort since the soul has heretofore not been spoken of in terms of faith and spirituality, the offer is made for you to skip what follows here and proceed directly onto the next chapter. It would be, however, in my estimation, a grave disservice to not at least offer a view of the bond between the soul and faith and how the absence of those things that maintain this connection causes a variety of difficulties many young people experience both within and outside the public schools of America. Through such understanding, it is possible to see one more aspect of the soul that is not only a possibility, but in the view of many people, myself included, a probability: that through a well-exercised and nurtured soul a person is able to come into touch with the wisdom and knowledge that God offers to the human species through that voice that is there within. Lacking this awareness and understanding or the outright refusal to consider this as a possibility limits access to that voice and denies us the opportunity to grow through its guidance. For the young people within the schools, the increasingly limited acknowledgement of the value of faith, religion and God confines them to reliance on things outside themselves with those consequences repeatedly cited herein that range from problematic to disastrous.

A LOSS OF FAITH...

The basis for the lack of inclusion of things of faith within the public schools has, according to those who are in opposition, solid grounding in the Constitution of the United States and the First Amendment's "establishment of religion" clause, which has come to mean a required separation between church and state, including the public schools. In the numerous disputes between the two opposing factions on this issue, those who argue for this separation speak to the rights of individuals not to have religious doctrine imposed upon them by the government,or in this case, by the schools. Those who argue that such divisive separation was not what the founding fathers had in mind, assert that the true intent was simply that the government should not be allowed to impose one particular form of religion on the citizenry; that the intent was not to effectively squelch any acknowledgement or recognition of a Supreme Being.

Because both sides are so ardent in their beliefs, there is not often an opportunity to break that particular section of the Constitution down to its simplest level and focus on the key words within. When those founding fathers spoke to the separation of church and state and to the prohibition of governmental establishment of a specified religion, they quite wisely did not use the term faith, rather they sought to provide for the freedom to practice faith in any way that an individual saw fit. There was no denial of faith in God or in spirituality; quite the opposite, they recognized the existence of a Supreme Being. We regularly verify our government's acknowledgement of God through the words of the Pledge of Allegiance and through those printed on the money we exchange daily. Politicians are not adverse to mention God and prayer in speeches, particularly in times of crisis. To pretend that the government is adverse to faith is simply unfounded--there is too much evidence to the contrary.

Somehow, however, we have moved to this time when including things of faith within the public schools has come to mean a violation of that particular clause of the Constitution. If we reconsider the historical trend towards things that are logical, rational and scientific, we can see that within the public schools, movement away from things of faith was the resultant consequence. We still had faith, it was just now placed in those things that could be observed and measured and explained. In the process, those outside voices grew louder and now spoke to the need to dismiss any visible entities that might demonstrate, illustrate or promote faith, such as inclusion of the Bible in literature classes, any type of school prayer, the teaching of Creationism or the establishment of any clubs or organizations that were in any way connected to spiritual belief. These could not be sponsored by the school, went the argument, because they violated that separation required by the Constitution. The world had come to a time when more and more of life's mysteries could be explained through logical and scientific means and so any opposing argument that there was still value in teaching, exposing or even allowing children access to things of faith fell on deaf ears, if it was even promoted at all. The outside voices of the world had effectively blurred the distinction between faith and religion, and the encouragement and inclusion of things of spirituality and faith in the schools rapidly declined.

Today we live in a world where educators worry about promoting faith within the public schools in terror of treading on ground that they have been regularly warned to avoid. The outside voices have gained increasing volume thanks to well-publicized court cases, such as the case of the portrait of Jesus Christ that was ordered removed from the hallway of a high school and other cases where schools were sued to prevent the inclusion of prayer in graduation ceremonies. Recently, states who had implemented laws to provide for a moment of silence for "voluntary prayer or meditation" have seen even such innocuous practices deemed unconstitutional on the grounds that such laws were, in essence, trying to reintroduce prayer into the public schools. No wonder those who are proponents of the inclusion of some acknowledgement of faith in the schools view it as an impossible battle. It would be nice to assume that there might be some middle ground, some balance to be attained, but it seems extremely unlikely and as such, our ability to educate students effectively is diminished in a variety of ways that deserve exploration.

A LOSS OF LEARNING...

There is a great deal that accompanies the loss of faith from our schools and perhaps the easiest place to begin is in the loss of learning that has accompanied the dismissal of things of faith from the education of our children. This initial consideration allows us to see some of the simplest implications arising from the determination to keep faith and the public schools very separate. One important result is the avoidance of allowing students access to things that might be seen as pertaining to God or to faith, such as the Bible, which receives limited coverage at best in the average public school of America. Yet the Bible has tremendous value in a wide range of areas, including its connection to so much of the literature that is typically found in a student's reading requirements throughout school.

When I was teaching English at the high school level, I constantly struggled with the inability my students seemed to have in drawing parallels between the works we were reading and stories or concepts from the Bible. I remember the first year I worked with students on Hemmingway's *The Old Man and the Sea,* only a handful of students out of the hundred or so in three sections could see the similarities drawn between the old man of the story and Christ. They couldn't understand when I referred to Santiago's young helper as a "disciple" or when I contrasted his three days at sea with Christ's entombment following the crucifixion. They had only minimal knowledge as to why Santiago's rope burns on his hands were so closely aligned with Christ's wounds from being nailed to the cross. Those students that could see the connection were lacking in their ability to discuss the numerous equivalents in too much depth, perhaps due to limited knowledge and perhaps equally due to their unwillingness to be seen as someone with a background of religious knowledge.   It wasn't just in this novel that similarities   to   Biblical   stories   were   found.   Whether in Steinbeck's *The Pearl*, Hawthorne's *The Scarlet Letter*, Dicken's *Tale of Two Cities*, or a wide range of other standard novels and short stories, Biblical parallels and allusions abound, and for students who had little or no previous knowledge to connect these to, the learning and growth they could experience was severely curtailed.

I must confess here that upon experiencing this early in my teaching career and discussing students' lack of such requisite knowledge with my more experienced colleagues, I heeded their advice and dismissed my inner voice which strongly suggested I provide my students with some Biblical stories so as to give them a basis for comparison prior to embarking on any literary undertakings, thereby enhancing their learning. It was just too risky, my colleagues insisted, and a parent might complain to the principal or the school board. Being a non-tenured teacher at that point who was interested in maintaining her career, I blundered onward and offered to students what I thought was the best I was allowed to give them. With that 20-20 hindsight we are always afforded, I now recognize that to avoid offering some type of Biblical reference point for the students to start their literary travels with was not in their best interest in terms of their ability to utilize the critical thinking that comes through the comparisons and contrasts that could be more effectively drawn with such background knowledge. This is but one price that we pay and our students in turn pay when we live in a world where schools are expected to be devoid of those things that speak to spirituality and faith.

In addition to the missing out on the sheer value of the Bible as a work of literature, the fear of its inclusion into English and literature classes has other implications as well.   It is often amazing, not to mention, discouraging, to see how much standard cultural knowledge is lost on American students due to their lack of knowledge of the Bible. I've worked with students who looked at me in utter confusion when I mention the "Golden Rule", comment that "You reap what you sow", or call someone a "Good Samaritan". They may have heard or even used the phrases, but have no concept as to their significance or origin, so with no background from which to draw, many of the common phrases and philosophies that are so much a part of our heritage are lost to our students. Likewise, the analogies and parables taught by Christ are missed, and missed by many of whom would be amazed at the significance of those stories, written so long ago, to the world they live in now. But they are without consistent opportunity to explore them in depth and with guidance. Outside voices and pressures will insist that this is the province of the church and the home and there is not disagreement here with that sentiment. I am, however, realistic enough to know that such opportunities range, for many students, from rare to non-existent. While it is a certainty that a great many students have opportunity to gain exposure to the Bible and its teachings through their various churches, a great many also have no such connection and lack what were, at one time, fairly standard references that derive from it.

AND A LOSS OF SOUL

The importance of the Bible in terms of its literary value and cultural knowledge is important, yet is has been offered, in all honesty, so as to offer some level of comfort to those who are still put off by the concept of the schools allowing for anything that might speak to faith or spirituality. It seeks to give some clear and acceptable logic for the incorporation of the Bible within the public schools at least as a work of literary value and thereby assuage those who would continue to argue against its inclusion. A more important point is that the acceptance of the Bible or moments of silence or prayer have potential soulful benefits as well. The central premise behind this book is one that encourages the nurturance of the souls of students, so to leave the reader without a clear picture of how the things of faith, such as the Bible or school prayer, provide for this would be essentially the same as not completing a promised journey and as such would be unfair.

In a world where we rely so heavily upon those things that are explainable and therefore understandable, there is also tremendous evidence that we are, as a nation, crying out for miracles or those things that are seemingly without rational cause. The proliferation over the past few years in movies, television programs and literature that concern miracles, spirituality, angels and yes, the soul, is evidence that we have perhaps subjugated this aspect of our being for long enough and it is now beginning to make itself known and felt once again. Yet in the world of academics, this resurgence of what can best be called things of faith is not readily accepted but is rather rejected with ferocity. These "things of faith",after all, cannot be seen, touched, smelled or in anyway proven through the measures available through scientific means, and cannot, therefore, be proven as real. Since we certainly wouldn't want to provide our students with something that could not be explained rationally and logically, we are safest to simply avoid such things all together and prevent students' exposure to them, or so it seems in the schools across this country. And this, despite the fact that an examination of such can offer no harm whatsoever and could possibly offer a variety of benefits, not the least of which would be a greater connection with the soul.

In an effort to most effectively empathize with the students that I serve and so as to best understand their thoughts and feelings, I will often seek to mentally place myself "in their shoes" and look at the world through their eyes and thereby gain a greater understanding and appreciation of the things that they think and feel and do.   We all have heard our adult counterparts at one time or another comment that they "wouldn't be a child for anything in the world these days", and such a phrase is not without solid grounding.   As noted earlier, we adults often forget all the small steps that were taken to reach the point that we are at today, and as such, we fail to recognize that all those same small steps necessary to the full development of a human's character and soul are much more treacherous steps today than they were in the past. The practice of mentally putting ourselves in the position of today's children and teenagers makes this realization much more possible.

With that thought in mind, you can return again to consider the movement of the schools over the past 40 to 50 years and the tremendous swing away from things of faith. It is unlikely that anyone will defend the notion that there is still an emphasis of any sort in this area, unless the person has been totally out of touch with the world around them for a significant period of time.   In putting ourselves in the shoes of our children and walking the path that they now walk, we can see that while the advancements made in science, in technology and in understanding the mysteries of the world around us has had tremendous benefits, there are fewer and fewer mysteries to explore in that world, and as such, we expect concrete and rational answers to everything that confronts us and we seek control over every facet of our lives. What's more, this place where we spend such a significant amount of time, the school, reinforces this notion by avoiding any mention or acknowledgement of faith, God or things that cannot be explained with scientific theory.

As children or teenagers facing complex mysteries that indeed have no clear cut answer or solutions, we find ourselves searching desperately outside ourselves for the provision of them and when they are not available or in evidence, those steps we are taking on the road to adulthood seem that much more perilous. We face the break-up of our family or the death of a parent and have no clear definition as to why it had to occur or how we are to cope. We go through the loss of friends and friendship and find ourselves bitter and angry and without the means to move past the negativity. We watch random acts of violence and terror and have no textbook to explain it or assure us that it won't happen to us. We go through the adolescent trials that make us feel different, alienated and alone, and have no point of reference to draw on for support and guidance. Even with all the technological gadgets and wizardry; even with all the rational, logical and scientific explanations available, none sufficiently can explain the deeply felt pain and confusion we experience in these and similar situations. The road of life we're on does indeed seem treacherous.

The fortunate among us have supportive homes and direction there and perhaps have a connection with the belief in God or a Supreme Being through which to draw comfort when dealing with both the simple and complex dilemmas that are faced in the process of growing up. But others of us have no connection. Though there was a time when not only was the acknowledgement of God more common in the homes of America, it was also more common in the schools as well and even the simple acknowledgement of faith in a power greater than our own and greater than those technological wonders of our making served to ease the discomfort during times of confusion, discouragement or sorrow.

We look again at our counterparts in childhood, adolescence and young adulthood. We are often dismayed and always disrupted by our companions who act out in the classroom. We attend the parties and watch people drink themselves into a stupor in an effort to "fit in". We watch our friends struggle with eating disorders in an obsessive desire to be thin and fit the proper image. We are horrified and forever changed when one of our classmates opts out of the journey by committing suicide. What we probably don't realize at this point in our lives is that all of these and the variety of other self-destructive acts that we and our peers engage in are simply means of seeking control in a world that has taught us since our earliest days that all things can be mastered by things outside ourselves that are logical, rational and explainable. But what we truly need at this point in our lives is the adult wisdom and acknowledgement that some things lie beyond our power to control or subvert or change, but through a faith in a power that lies not only outside us but inside us, in our souls, as well, we can trust that even our worst difficulties and trials will eventually be found to have a solution.

Stepping out of the shoes of our children now we can return to the earlier observation that, particularly within the academic world of American schools, that type of adult wisdom is difficult to come by. That one place where we can virtually assure that the majority of American children will attend at some point is effectively precluded from offering children any acknowledgement that there just may be a power greater than our own in guiding and directing the world and its people. School prayer is banned. Christian student groups have difficulty using school facilities. Graduation prayer and baccalaureate services vanish. Teaching the Bible simply as literature is frowned upon. The peripheral education that our children receive through all this is that there is no value in placing faith in God. Even those administrators and teachers who have profound influence on the young people they work with and who may well have personal convictions of faith, fail to vocalize such beliefs for the fear of the harsh retributions that may follow. Instead they offer "sound, practical and logical" lessons to children who more and more are confused and terrified by a world that seems increasingly meaningless to them.

And so we return to the soul. A majority of Americans believe in the existence of God, despite there being no "scientific evidence" to prove it. The existence of a soul as a part of a human being is equally without scientific proof and is even a difficult concept to define in concrete terms and is less likely to be accepted as anything other than a religious theory. With the knowledge that the academic world essentially refuses to allow admittance of a commonly accepted God within the schools, you start to understand that the chance of the soul being acknowledged, exercised and nurtured overtly and consciously with in the classrooms of America is slight. It would simply be one more concept too closely aligned with religion that would press that separation between church and state. So we dismiss things of faith, and the soul falls into the mix of what is discarded. In the process, however, we are also discarding an entity that might effectively serve to help alleviate the confusion, despair, hopelessness and lack of feeling displayed by an increasing number of American youth.

Whether or not the soul is a religious entity is not the issue here, nor is this an intended battle cry meant to rally Christian forces to more effectively push for the inclusion of The Bible, prayer or other things of faith within the schools. It is, however, a cry for balance and a plea to return to the schools the freedom to recognize those things that are mysterious and without explanation, including the soul. The benefits to acknowledging and taking care of the soul far outweigh the real or perceived risks taken with the inclusion of things of faith within the schools.

Though the benefits of the well-exercised and nurtured soul was discussed at some length earlier, one more of particular importance requires some additional emphasis to offer one final consideration as to the importance of the schools' allowance for faith in the unknown and unexplained. A fairly familiar term at this point will be that of man's inner voice, that being the voice of the soul, which was said to have the key to right and wrong. Additional discussion has been offered as to how diligently and effectively the outside voices of the world around us seek to drown out that voice, often for purely economic reasons.

I discussed this idea a while back with a friend who was not adverse to the concept of the soul, but who didn't accept the belief that through the voice of the soul, a human could have access to those answers that would put us on the correct paths in life. If such was the case, he asserted, then why would Adam and Eve have fallen from grace? "After all," he said, "There weren't a lot of outside voices drowning out the voice of their souls."

"What would you consider the serpent to be?" I asked.

There are a large number of similar serpents in the world around us and around the students who attend American schools today, and as noted, they effectively drown out the voice of the soul and hinder the ability to hear the wisdom and knowledge that is present there. Carl Jung referred to a "collective unconscious",[1] or a universally held collection of thoughts, understandings, images and knowledge that was an inherent part of all humans. Whether this is called the soul, the psyche or the inner voice makes no difference. It is still that part of a human that has the innate ability to determine both the most simple and the most complex issues of right and wrong. It is as well that part which provides us with our intuitions and our feelings. From these arise our principles and convictions from which we derive a consistent behavior and manner of living--if we are in close connection with the soul. The serpents in our world today, including those which press for disavowal of anything of faith within the schools, dislike trust in that collective unconscious and encourage what might appropriately be called a collective conscious, through which the entire human society believes only in those things that are tangible and explainable. If they succeed, we are effectively made reliant on those things that lie outside ourselves for both direction in life and solutions to life's problems and we fall victim to the inherent troubles that follow when we depend on things which are costly, which don't always work and which can be lost in the blink of an eye. We are without a solid foundation of principles and convictions through which we can derive our behavior and we thus will be dependent upon that collective conscious for direction. We are effectively crippled by all this dependence, but even this crippling often serves to make us just more reliant on something else outside ourselves.

For the young people in schools today this push away from trust in the collective unconscious, the soul or the inner voice is crippling them as well. Those who are the furthest from a connection with their soul have become so reliant on things outside themselves that they are angry, dissatisfied and hostile and the world is seeing and feeling the result. There are few, if any, places where they are encouraged to heed the inner voice of their soul and to trust its guidance and direction so they too are without the principles and convictions that would serve to guide their behavior. Worse, they are still at a stage of development where everything is a lesson, and this lesson reinforces the notion of depending on things outside of themselves. It's as if they have not only been provided with crutches that are well-intentioned devices to help them walk, they have been encouraged to rely on these and dismiss any value in their natural ability to walk unaided. Such a violation of nature goes against the grain as children thus crippled feel their ability to cope, to trust themselves, to even survive, is dependent upon something outside themselves over which they have, in reality, little control. It's not surprising that they are angry. It is the expected result of the refusal to acknowledge anything that can't be understood through logical, rational means, including the wisdom to be found in the soul.

Though returning things of faith back within the schools could be easily accomplished, it seems an unlikely occurrence and in many ways this is not hard to understand. When you step back and listen to both those in favor of such a return and those ardently opposed, it is hard not to be struck by the ferocity with which they both espouse their points of view. I can well appreciate any school district's unwillingness to incur the wrath of either side for fear of what might transpire in terms of protests, legal action and the like. Yet I often conceptualize the soul as that entity through which God speaks to humankind and offers the direction and guidance so needed in the world today. In conceptualizing this, and in recognizing that 98% of our society claim belief in God, one has to wonder how we can remain so unwilling to find the balance within the schools that would allow for students to reach and maintain that vital connection with that inner voice of their souls.

PART III

Making the Decision to Return to the Soul

I t is hard to dam up a raging river that has the pressure of thousands of gallons of water propelling it forward, and damming up the current flow of education is, likewise, a daunting task, particularly if the reason for altering the flow is to provide for an unproven, unresearched entity such as the soul. And while the foregoing has offered a definition as to why the course of education should return to a semblance of balance and has sought to include the means by which it could be accomplished, there is still the unanswered question as to why it is not being done and why making such a change will be so difficult.

Nothing in what has gone before this should indicate that it is only the youth of our society that have been moved and educated away from a connection with soul. Indeed, for all of us, the movement of the world and the society over the past decades has been one that has precluded many, if not most, of us from remaining solidly in touch with our souls. For those of us in adulthood, now making the decisions that affect others including the students in American schools, this trend away from the soul is one that has had profound implications on the way in which we reach decisions and on what impacts the policies that we put into place.

It is a frightening reality, the vicious circle in which we find ourselves. On the whole, we educators truly wish to seek the best means to educate the children in our schools. We care about them and love them. Yet there are so many outside forces and voices that have educated and continue to educate us that it is difficult to discern what is truly the best path to take. This may well be due to the reality that it is not only the children in the schools, but the decision-makers as well, who are suffering from a loss of connection with soul.

Perhaps a brief poem that I penned during one educational meeting can summarize it best.

There is no soul within this place.
It's absence is apparent on every face
as around the table in well-lit gloom
they plot the future, as well their doom.

A spectator to this meeting of minds
my soul feels grief at what it finds.
They determine the futures of those they teach
and assume their souls lie out of reach.

So these, the brilliant, the knowing, the wise,
teach children that life-long happiness lies
in work-place skills and material gain.
Though the body may thrive, the soul's in pain.

How sad for those who trust us so
to teach them all they'll need to know.
We've failed to see them each as whole
as we teach to their intellect and neglect their soul.

CHAPTER 9

The Making of Educational Decisions

Within the schools of America decisions are made on a daily basis and while this is a given, the manner in which many of these decisions are often made is one that deserves exploration and examination. In doing so, it is easier to see how our schools, truly microcosms of the society that houses them, have come to fully reflect the world around us and how this world impacts what we, and therefore our children and students, see, hear, learn and come to believe. If you want to see what a society views as important in life, step into the schools. Likewise, if you wish to see the way in which a society believes decisions should be reached, the schools can provide such education. It seems important to do this and to see as clearly and vividly as possible how much impact the outside voices of this world truly have on education; not just in the question of how our young people should be educated, but also in how they have educated and influenced those who directly teach our children.

I mentioned at the outset of this book that writing this was an answer to the grief that I often felt as I participated in one meeting after another in which I watched those things that would foster soul be eradicated from the curriculum. I sought a variety of means to educate fellow staff that we were doing a disservice to our students by eliminating courses and requirements in the creative areas while increasing the demands in the intellectual realm, in those areas that were so well designed to make them effective workers. I certainly knew enough not to mention the term "soul" to my colleagues who would not be willing to even attempt to conceptualize something as non-tangible as the soul as anything other than a purely religious and theoretical concept. I should add here, as many of my colleagues will tell you, I often went about this attempted education in an ineffective, albeit, well-meaning manner. In all reality, though, how can you explain this to others whose rational and logical minds truly, honestly and in sincere interest of those students they serve, believe firmly that the best they can do for children is to help them on the road to economic self-sufficiency? How can you deny these as good intentions when all the illustrations to be had, whether in television, in words from powerful business executives, in fact, from the entire society around them cry out that American children cannot compete with their foreign counterparts; that those students in American schools are going to lose out in the growing global village that we are creating?

Yet as I worked with struggling children, as I listened to stories of home lives that made me cringe, as I watched children rebel and fight and suffer within the schools, I slowly grew to realize that those having the greatest difficulty, those that I worked with the most, were the ones who were severely lacking in the ability to hear the wisdom of their inner voice--their soul--and even in the best and brightest of students this was also creating problems. The certainty of this, like the soul itself, was and remains as something difficult to put into tangible terms, yet I felt driven to educate my colleagues, not to encourage soul related pursuits and learning to the exclusion of the other areas, but to return to some semblance of balance between the two. But even as I pursued this, I realized I was on an uphill battle against all those forces of the outside world that had been effectively educating all of us for decades. What's more, like John in *Brave New World*, the struggle against all those outside forces and voices was a tremendous effort. I remember a band director in high school telling the joke of the student in the marching band who boasted that he was on the right foot while the rest of the marchers were out of step, and like that student and like Huxley's John, it was difficult to determine whether I was totally out of step with the world around me. I often underwent deep bouts of self-doubt, wondering if all of those outside voices that denied the wisdom I was hearing from my own soul were right and I was crazy. But even as I would question and ponder whether I was going through some strange mental delusions, something would occur that would confirm that I was not crazy and should stay the course.

Perhaps an example here will serve better than my somewhat vague explanations and descriptions. Shortly after I realized that I was in the midst of a tremendous swim upstream in attempting to educate my colleagues on this idea and had found myself embroiled in writing a book that might do it better than I was verbally able, I became involved in an conversation with a co-worker. A well-intentioned sort, he began the conversation with a comment about what good work I was doing as an administrator and in working with children. The conversation digressed from there.

"You have very strong convictions about what's best for children," he commented.

"We're here to serve kids," I replied, simply. "And I do have some strong beliefs. I guess I just wish that others could see that many of the things that we're doing are not in our students' best interest."

From there we discussed many of the current trends, including those that were being implemented in our district and I questioned their value and whether these changes would be truly best for children or in reality, best and most convenient for the adults around them.

My colleague, with anger growing at my questioning of those things he was in support of, commented that he truly admired my convictions and in fact, wished that he had as strong a belief, but then concluded with, "The bottom line, Tammi, is that these strong convictions of yours could get in the way of what we're trying to do, and we can't have you holding on to them."

While this is only one part of a long and dismal conversation, it occurred just that way and I found myself thinking, "Do you hear what you're saying?! You can't have me holding on to my convictions?! Even as you say I do a good job in working with children, which is an outgrowth of those very convictions?!!!" Yet even as these thoughts raced through my brain, I could feel self-doubt and self-distrust seeping into my brain and I ended up driving home in tears, again struggling with the question as to whether I was the marcher who thought she was the only member of the band who was in step.

To make a long story somewhat shorter, I went home, intending to work on my writing but couldn't get my focus. I had purchased, three months earlier, a copy of M. Scott Peck's book, *Further Along the Road Less Traveled*, but had never read it, intending to purchase a copy of his first, *The Road Less Traveled*, and read them in sequence in my usual organized way. But I decided to violate one of my usual patterns of behavior so I settled down on the couch and began to read, until I came to the section, "The Agony of Not Knowing". In this section, Peck speaks to the difficulty that surrounds us when we do not know whether we are pursuing the right path, commenting on his own struggles when he questioned whether his decision to go into public speaking was an "ego trip". He identified his desire for an easy formula, some revelation, to answer that question for him. Yet as Peck notes, there is no formula for guaranteeing that what we are doing or saying or thinking is correct. "Each instance is different, each is unique, and each time, if you are seeking the truth, you have to ask the question. Should you do this you will likely come to the correct decision, but you will also have to put up with the pain of not knowing for sure."[1] Even as I read this, I felt as if a weight had been lifted. It was alright not to know with absolute certainty if my convictions were right, but I had to, none the less, trust that they were. I had to listen to the wisdom of my soul, which my colleague as well as the world and those outside voices around me would prefer I not do.

I include this story for a couple of reasons. First and foremost, the co-worker with whom I had that conversation was a well-meaning, well-intentioned educator who was truly interested in what was best for children. Like all of the world around him though, he had been effectively educated by the outside voices and believed what they had taught, so if work-place skills and education in the intellectual realm was the lesson that they were preaching, that's what he believed and that was the path that he followed. He could be less unsure and less concerned than I simply due to the fact that he was, at least, in step with everyone else. Unlike him though, I had, over the course of my life, come to trust that inner voice. It had never steered me wrong and though I might be faced with someone who wanted me to abandon the convictions and principles that arose from that inner voice of my soul, I needed to remember that there wouldn't be, as Peck so accurately pointed out, any formula for knowing I was correct in staying the path. All I could do was hold onto those convictions and live by them, and all the while put up with the pain of not knowing with absolute certainty that I was doing the right thing.

Out of all this came the further realization that since the vast majority of the populace had been educated in the same manner as my colleague, including those in the field of education, they too were so effectively conditioned by what those outside of themselves were saying and thinking, that they had lost their ability to hear their own inner voice. Like him, they were not concerned that they were on the wrong path because so many others were traveling the same one. When this was taken into consideration alongside the growing societal emphasis on those work-place skills and the trend towards education in the intellectual realm to the exclusion of education in the simply enjoyable and creative, the realization of why I was in such a difficult swim upstream became even more clear. As this awareness dawned, so too did the certainty that unless some voice found a way to break through all that outside rabble to remind educators to examine their own hearts and souls to discover what they truly believe is best for children, those voices of the outside world would gain further strength in teaching our children their very self-serving definitions of what is most valuable in this world. As we are seeing more and more with each passing day, much of this is not only without value, it is also damaging to children.

Another thing also came clear following that particular conversation and that was the fear that is generated by a pattern of thought, beliefs or convictions that are out of step with the current norms. When someone or something challenges the learning that has come from years of indoctrination, it is seen as a tremendous threat and threats invariably generate both fear and anger. Remember the analogy of the child who is taught two plus two equals three will come to believe it if it is prevalent and pervasive and is taught by the most influential people in his life.

Attempts to educate him otherwise will be met by anger and fear. Educators find themselves in a similar situation. Whether wisdom from the government, admonitions from business and industry, pleas from parents and taxpayers or their own upbringing, everything around them has convinced them that the business of education is to prepare children for the economic world around them and the dog-eat-dog world they will enter. To do otherwise or to even attempt to modify this current status quo would, they believe, create a large amount of anger and fear among those powerful forces, and educators are loathe to do this, so dependent are they on the money and goodwill to be had there.

Too, as with my colleague, there is that fear and anger that is generated among educators themselves when they are questioned or challenged as to the manner in which they are conducting their work. They have heeded the logical demand from society and have increased the emphasis on teaching in the intellectual areas, becoming quite comfortable that they are operating as the world sees fit. They shut down any questioning that arises by displaying anger and righteous indignation. After all, they are working their best at meeting the demands of an increasingly complex society. As long as no true challenges arise, their mode of education retains its status and power. As this has proceeded, however, we have also forgotten that when we are talking about elementary and secondary education, we are talking about educating children and there is much more to those children and their lives than simply moving into the world of work; namely educating them to have time as children and to develop the capacity to become happy and whole adults. With the current status quo, throwing this idea up to educators for consideration is to be met with either anger, disgust or, as will be looked at shortly, alienation and censure.

It is very possible that people might think that this whole concept of educating children to be happy and whole is not what business and industry, the government or anyone else is concerned with, yet what do the reports from business and industry cite? What concern does the government report when it is talking about the problems of young people? What do schools struggle against in increasing numbers? Through business and industry we hear that one of the biggest problems with workers is in their inability to work cooperatively with others. From the government we hear of increasing worries about juvenile crime and delinquency. And schools scramble to discover the means to meet the needs of those students who are slipping through the cracks and either mentally or physically dropping out of the educational system. In schools across this country, there may well be a trend to encourage logic and the teaching of critical thinking, but it seems that in believing we have created a successful system by more and more educating almost solely to the intellectual and logical with the corresponding dismissal of the creative and intuitive, we demonstrate neither logic nor evidence of critical thought. After all, what helps a child learn how to work cooperatively with others better than in the group creation of a choral performance, a band concert, a theatrical production or a sports team? What better way to lower the number of students involved in crime and delinquency than to work at teaching them the means for positive creation? How can you better keep students in school than by making it a place that meets their needs and one in which they are loved, accepted and able to find their own definitions of success? To convince the outside voices of this is difficult if not impossible, as it diminishes the value of those things that they have worked to impress upon the world as important. Educators are no different than anyone else in this.

They are not likely to look favorably, but more likely with anger, upon anything that impinges on some long-held, firmly-established beliefs.

COLLABORATION AND TEAMING IN EDUCATIONAL DECISIONS

It's always fun and instructive to move among the shelves of a bookstore and see the various titles in print on an array of topics. Invariably, a trip through a bookstore can reveal what the current trends are in fiction, in philosophy, in self-help or in business. One of the most popular modes found in business and industry which is verified in literature currently on the market is in the area of group process and group decision-making. You can find any number of books either explaining the why's of this type of process, containing illustrations on how to achieve group consensus in effective ways, or telling the stories of tremendously profitable corporations which utilize such approaches. What you are less likely to find are any books supporting the concept of individualism and the value of the individual and his ideas to the organization. This idea was looked at in Chapter 3 as it related to students but it relates as well to the organization and decision making in our public schools.

Today's popular wisdom is to achieve total group consensus, to have all levels of an organization participate in the decision-making and, though not said in so many words, to avoid making waves if you have a different opinion or belief. As with most popular trends and ideas, there is merit in the concept of the group process and collaborative decision making. There is far too much evidence to support its use to discount its value to any organization. It is simply another example of that axiom that when you see a tremendous increase in one area you are bound to find a correlational decrease in another. In this case, our society has increased the emphasis in group teaming and decision-making and has seen a resultant decrease in the recognition of the value of individuality. While it was earlier noted how, historically, people who did not conform to the commonly held beliefs of their era made important contributions to their world and time, today in education as in the society at large, any voice that seeks to put forth an idea which is different and distinct from that held by the group is drowned out by a collectively powerful voice and the value of the individual thought has much less chance of making entrance into that group decision-making process. It is possible that some very worthwhile ideas never see the light of day precisely for that reason.

Returning then to the idea of education and the educational decisions that are being made across this country, we struggle with how best to educate children so as to not only improve the future of our nation and society, but also to seek the means to move growing numbers of youth past the problems that they are facing as they mature. Education and educational policy makers, whether in government or in the school districts themselves follow societal trends, usually in a big way. Any educator who has been in the business for any length of time can speak to the variety of societal fads and fashions that they have seen come and go, to a point that many have become jaded when some new idea or theory comes on to the scene. One of the current trends is this collaborative teaming, shared decision-making, group process, or whatever name it may be given. Tied into this trend are the pressures and demands being placed upon the schools by business and industry, by the government and by the tax-paying public. When the schools pair these two factors, the result is districts being run via that shared decision-making, in which the group members have all been educated and conditioned by the outside voices of our world. They are groups which when formed are well-meaning, intelligent, logical and intellectual; who base their educational decisions on that logic and intellect and current research.

Much of the educational research being done currently is in the benefits of teaching students in the areas of intellectual thought and technology and to prepare them for the work force. Now I view this research with at least a small amount of skepticism. While I believe that there is basis in fact for much of it, I also review history to recognize that it is possible to conduct research so as to support anything you want it to support, at least for a while. If you doubt this, remember that the tobacco industry has research that dismisses connections between smoking and cancer, or that there was research that supported the safety of radiation and various pesticides.

As educational groups then work in their sincere effort to do the best for children, they are seriously influenced by such research and they use it to support their decisions and the resultant manner in which students are educated. I often question what would, and hopefully will, happen when research begins to be conducted on the need for children to have exercise and development of their souls and when these studies offer convincing evidence that such needs to occur. My guess is that, in typical bandwagon effect, the educational world would jump on it and we would see an increase in that area with a correlational decrease in the intellectual realm. This too would be unfortunate since the whole premise is that there needs to be a balance between the two in order to most effectively educate the whole child, who needs both the intellectual and the soul development.

All of this being the case, as the educational decisions are made, all of these factors come into play. The outside voices of the world having effectively done their job in educating those who make decisions in the schools, the manner in which children are educated is likewise determined by those outside voices and we have today's results where we see that strong emphasis in math, science, technology and workplace skills and the de-emphasis in the soulful areas. The potential for anyone to fight against this very powerful movement is minimal, as the forces against it are so strong and, again, there is much validity in what they are seeking to teach children. Yet, as in working with students, I find it interesting how often educators will verify the importance of teaching in the creative, more soul-nurturing areas only to follow such comments with a, *"But* we have to prepare them for the work place," or *"But* there's not enough time in the day." It's interesting how those outside voices intrude on everyone, not only our students.

Though we may well, through our instincts, intuitions and inner voices, realize that allowing our students to grow in the creative, soul-nurturing areas is important, we are providing for it less and less and the result has meant less satisfied, less happy students.   This is verified by a comment made by various educational theorists who in speeches and in writings will note that almost 100% of the children in kindergarten classrooms say they enjoy school, which is compared with 65% who report the same at the junior high or middle school level with only 30% reporting to enjoy school by the time they enter high school. This is usually followed up with a joke of sorts, referring to the fact that high school educators blame it on the junior high or middle school staffs; these in turn point to the elementary levels and those at the elementary levels in turn blame the parents. The joke concludes with a question as to whom the parents can, in turn blame, with the assumption being that they are the ones that should ultimately bear the guilt of student dissatisfaction with school. I would offer that where to place the blame should not be the issue for those of us in the schools or anywhere else; rather the question should address how we can best return childhood, innocence and soulfulness to our children and lessen or remove that dissatisfaction.

I am uncomfortable with any type of blame game and particularly one such as that noted since it serves no purpose in improving the educational lives of children; it only seeks to find fault. As we continue to operate in our group mode of decision-making, this type of blame placing is very common. It is one of the things that groups do, especially in the absence of strong leadership so often missing under group consensus modes. I once commented to a supervisor that such complaining and blaming wasted an inordinate amount of time in education and really served no purpose, to which he responded that the staff needed a certain amount of time to air their griefs, gripes and grievances and that it was a healthy and beneficial aspect of the group process. As this occurs, however, the end result tends to be less than beneficial and certainly less than healthy. During such occasions, the group cements its belief that education is difficult, stressful and complicated and this in turn further cements the belief that any simple solutions to the problems that they are facing can not possibly have any value or any merit. After all, if their jobs are so complex, surely only the most complex solutions will make it better. That seems only logical.

But the soul craves simplicity, not only the souls of our students but also the souls of the adults making the decisions in our schools. The children who they are working with and who move into the world of public education at the age of five or six thrive on simplicity and model this soul need well. They revel in the creativity, the freedom and the beauty that they so naturally find in the things that they are asked to do. Their souls are being nurtured and because they are still children who have not yet been unalterably conditioned by the world around them, they can still tap into their inner voices. We can all think of times when, with pure, unabashed innocence, a child said something of such profound wisdom that we laughed in sheer delight. This natural freedom and soulfulness is a lesson that our youngest students have to offer those making decisions in the schools. Through the early grades, the soulfulness and creative areas to develop it may still be intact and our children still happy. But as we lay out their path through the educational system, less and less is retained that speaks to simplicity, creativity, freedom and beauty. By the time high school is reached, students are faced with a gauntlet to run of immensely complex dimensions and the things that serve to exercise and nurture the soul have been relegated to a position of relative unimportance. After all, in educators' minds, to merely develop a balance between the creative and intellectual realm is much too simple an idea to actually have any possibility of addressing all of these complex problems facing the schools and the students within them.

So rather than learning from our youngest, most soulful members of the educational world, those making decisions and policy depend on the research which is overwhelmingly focused in the area of intellectual and technological growth. In doing so, decisions are made and students are pushed into developing greater skills and competencies in these areas, at earlier and earlier grades. As this maintains its position as the prevailing school of thought, there is little wonder that the schools indeed do face increasingly complex and frightening problems with the children who it seeks to educate. It has all the trappings of a self-fulfilling prophesy.

In looking at this whole idea of how decisions are made, the creation of another circle is seen. As schools step up their curricular demands in the intellectual and technical areas, the lives of the educators become, in all reality, more complex. They are required to develop new skills, to learn new methods and to find different strategies to effectively teach these things. They find themselves frazzled and burned out, feeling overworked, underpaid and in general, without a great deal of support from the world around them that still expresses dissatisfaction with how students are educated. These educators then come together to collaboratively determine the best approach in working to meet the complex demands of their professions and are validated by their colleagues that their jobs are tough, difficult and complicated. They team this with periodic complaints that the students that are coming into the schools are not what they once were in terms of their willingness to be compliant and follow the dictates given them. They bemoan the fact that the disciplinary problems are horrendous. All of this further fuels their belief that their job is an elaborate and complicated one which calls for the most elaborate and complicated of solutions. They see and implement potential solutions, appropriately complex and demanding, that are sold effectively by the outside voices of the world which claims that they will make things better. In reality, these solutions only serve to complicate the job and make it even tougher. Not only is the job itself more difficult, but the students, in rebelling against this complexity which so violates the needs of their soul, act up, assume the hardships and complexity of the world around them and the result is increased disciplinary problems and decreased mental and physical retention. So the educators see their jobs as complex...I think you get the picture.

There are a number of points that should be made about the examination of this particular vicious circle. I mentioned earlier that those who move against the status quo meet with alienation and censure. For an individual or individuals to break into the vicious circle identified here and to attempt to illustrate how non-productive the movement of this circle is would engender anger on the part of those so caught up in it. Even those who are caught in such a cycle experience fear and anger when the futility of the behaviors found there is put into perspective. When fear and anger are experienced, there is a shutting down and an unwillingness to hear, let alone accept, any alternate thought.

Couple this with the fact that those things that might actually benefit students and staff in breaking out of the circle are very simple in concept and in practice and you totally shut down any chance of acceptance. It is just too simple to actually work. To use a popular term these days, you are encouraging a paradigm shift of immense proportions that they are unable to make. To suggest a change in their thinking is to invalidate all those things that they have been learning, believing and implementing with what they believe is great hardship and difficulty on their part. They are supported in this inability by all of those caught with them thanks in part to that collaborative process that encourages the development of a group mentality and discourages individualism and individual thought.

While this whole group process is the prevailing method of operation, not only within the schools but also in the world at large, there are those people that may recognize the value and benefits derived from it, but who also balance it with the recognition of the value of the individual and the value of individual thought. In the realm of business, these are the ones who create tremendously successful products or concepts that others scoffed at initially, saying they couldn't be done. In the realm of education, these often tend to be those educators who work diligently at establishing a positive climate for the children within their classes, who find creative and imaginative means to teach the requisite lessons and who work to allow students the room to develop their own individuality and uniqueness. I have been privileged to know a number of such teachers but the one who perhaps most exemplified this whole idea was Katie, a social studies teacher at the high school where I worked.

Katie was one of those highly successful teachers who kept a very low profile. Diminutive and quiet, she didn't radiate power or control, rather a self-effacing image that belied the strength of her influence on students. Not studied nor overtly practiced, Katie's teaching style was one that incorporated the wholeness of her students into each lesson that she presented. She modeled tranquility and calm, never yelling at or berating her students, and disciplinary problems within her classroom were virtually non-existent, though she taught primarily ninth grade students in a required class.

I spoke with Katie a year or so ago regarding her success in the classroom and why she felt she was so effective with her students.

She had laughed pleasantly at the question as to how she learned to work so well with students. "I always remember that they're children," she said. "And not mini-adults."

"There's more to it than that," I said. "You teach three sections of a freshman social studies class and have no discipline problems. The failure rate of your students is extremely low and what's more, when I observe your classes, they always seem to be having fun and enjoying what they're doing."

"We all have things that we want and need," she answered. "Our students are no different than any one else. I simply work to make sure that in my classroom and within my lessons, I am always working to meet those things that the kids need. They do all the work from there."

Katie was one of those educators who, despite her successes in the classroom, tended to remain fairly quiet within those collaborative meetings where complexity is the order of the day. Instead, she would return to her classrooms following one of these meetings and operate with a measure of simplicity and freedom that was accepted and appreciated by her students. She intrigued me, as do similar educators because, regardless of the subject area, level of education or grade level taught, they are invariably admired by their colleagues for their easy-going demeanor and their success with students. They also tend to be unable to cite one particular reason for their ability to work so effectively with children, but will speak to meeting children at their level and allowing students the opportunity to make choices and to work with materials and activities that they enjoy. They will talk about trying to make sure that the learning is fun and relevant. They often refer, as Katie did, to planning lessons to meet all the needs of their students. It is interesting to note on this last that these teachers will often cite educational theorists like Abraham Maslow or William Glasser to support this particular concept, and may do so to justify their success with a research base. Yet anyone who enters a truly successful classroom will observe that even those teachers who have only a passing knowledge of such theorists instinctively operate in a manner that meets all the needs of their students. Through their methods, these teachers, without conscious realization, are also meeting the need for the souls within their students to be nurtured and exercised. In these classrooms, you find the opportunities for self-reliance, the activities of creation, a high degree of simplicity and all those other elements so craved by the soul. There is little wonder then why these teachers, when faced with the child who acts up and causes difficulty in the classroom down the hall, experience virtually no similar problems.

Put this type of teacher now into a group situation as was noted earlier and the simplicity of this manner of working with children is diminished. It may be recognized and acknowledged, but is colored by the mind-set that often comes with the group process. I have sat in any number of meetings in which I heard reference to the fact that "Education won't always be fun," or "I'm not paid to entertain students." Those harboring such views tend to be very sure of what they are saying having given it little if any individual thought or consideration, rather blending in with those who are like-minded. Their sheer numbers make them loud and powerful voices. It has almost amused me at times to watch how a group mind-set can give rise to what might best be called a "hardship mentality" and the flow of the meeting in which simple ideas are presented moves from the truth that learning for both children and adults should be simple and fun, and turns to the complaints that the business of education is difficult, challenging and tedious. Before long, those teachers like Katie have quieted and chosen not to fight against this powerful flow of hardship. They return to their classrooms and operate quietly in their own way with which they see clear success.

I say that this has almost amused me at times but I should confess that more often than not I felt an anger and a grief as I watched the flow of such meetings. It is nothing more than a continuation of a circle that is non-productive and non-successful. The individuals who may voice something out of step with the popularly held thoughts and beliefs of hardship see as improbable the movement of the group from the vicious circle that they are caught up in. They and their ideas are shut down by those who create a sense of importance and value out of being able to complain, worry and become stressed over the difficulty of the job they have to do and these are validated mightily through that group process. Anyone who seeks to dismiss this hardship or break it down to its most simple level that would allow for movement past it, is often alienated from the group and shut down in a most effective way.

This leads back to the bottom line of education and educational decisions: the children that those of us in education are paid to teach. The children are the victims in this vicious circle in a number of ways. First and foremost, it was noted earlier that children learn much more than just the educational material that they are presented with, learning and adopting as well the attitudes and beliefs that are modeled by those around them. They listen to the stories of how tough and demanding education is and how complex the world of work is, not only from the media and others, but also within their classrooms where they spend such a large part of their lives. There is some sad irony in the fact that they are so regularly instructed in the necessity and importance of developing skills to move into the world of work by many whom model and discuss how stressful and complex their own jobs are. It is almost enough to encourage students not to learn the skills necessary to move into a job or career, so unpleasant and stressful does that eventuality often seem. There is little around to illustrate that learning, growing or working needn't be complex and stressful.

Likewise, through modeling and through the prevailing mode of operation within the society and within the schools, they are made to work in cooperative groups to a greater and greater extent, and as this happens, the value of their individual thought is minimized. As this vital part of themselves is devalued, they come to trust their inner voice less and less to the point that they are almost solely reliant on thoughts, beliefs and ideas from outside themselves, instead seeking validation through others. As this reliance gains strength and they exhibit greater and greater trust in those outside voices, they are more readily swayed into following along with whatever those voices suggest. And when those little images of the angel and devil cited earlier appear on their shoulders, they follow along with message of the latter, because all they have learned from both the outright education and the peripheral education all around them is that they should not heed the other--the voice of their soul.

All of this is simply one more arc of a vicious circle that is in full swing and while there may be questions as to where it truly started or who or what is to blame, these are irrelevant. The circle is and will continue to exist until we return to valuing the wholeness and completeness of those children within the classrooms of America and make decisions to incorporate the soul-needs of simplicity, freedom, creativity, belonging, nature and faith. Lacking this, those of us in education will continue to further complicate the already complicated task of teaching children and many of those who are the recipients of this complexity, loss of self-reliance and lack of freedom within the world of education will rebel, make for further complications and a guaranteed continuation of this circle in which we are all so caught.

—— CHAPTER 10 ——

Traveling the Path Towards the Return to the Soul

A friend of mine who works as a high school counselor has often referred to himself as a "freedom fighter for kids". I never truly appreciated the significance of that phrase until I started to research and develop an understanding of the soul and its importance in allowing us to be happy and whole individuals. Though he would perhaps not term the methods he uses to work with students through their difficulties as "soul work", he effectively coaches them how to release the inappropriate, inaccurate or outright damaging lessons that they have been taught over the years by their experiences. As they do this, they are better able to come into touch with their souls and find the beauty, joy and freedom that life has to offer. In short, they become happier and more complete individuals. In essence, that is what has been offered throughout this book--a means to provide for the students moving through American schools a chance at freedom from all those things that so effectively prevent it.

There is certainly some value to those things that are currently being stressed in education and that has not been a point of dispute here. The cry is for a movement towards balance and the need for our children to have other things, such as education in the creative and intuitive realm, which have value and importance but which more and more lose out because the voices in their support are being drowned out. I wouldn't want to leave anyone with the notion that a majority of educators see no value in these. In fact, most will testify to their value and importance to children. But they are most often seen as areas of development that the students within their classrooms can attain either through their homes and families, or through extra curricular areas. They sincerely believe that if they are to do justice to those technological and intellectual areas of pursuit, more of their time as educators should be devoted to this end and that the other areas will be developed elsewhere. Yet as more and more American youth are raised in dysfunctional homes and more and more are educated away from being able to trust their inner voices, that "elsewhere" that students may get the exercise for their soul is difficult for many to find.

Stop for a moment and think about humankind. We readily accept the workings of the human body, so intricate and complex. Science has given us concrete evidence and data as to the location, functioning, health and well-being of our various organs and systems and so, being tangible and observable, value is given. Likewise, credence is given to the workings of the mind and the intellect, perhaps because these are housed and make themselves apparent through another tangible entity, the brain. While all of these are undeniable aspects of the human animal, they fail to take into account some equally real aspects of the species.

Reflect for a moment on a human's ability to feel joy when facing a beautiful sunset, the swell of pride that comes following a positive creation, the warmth experienced in moments of love and friendship, and the peace that we experience in those quiet times when everything seems right with the world. To credit these and the variety of other feelings and emotions we encounter on a regular basis solely to the physical, observable systems of the human body fails to explain why they occur.

True, the work of psychologists and psychiatrists will speak to this, but their words will more likely credit some past experience for the emotion so as to be able to offer the tangible and logical explanation, but if you think even deeper, you still have to question why. Why is it that I feel so calm and peaceful when I take a walk in a quiet forest? What is happening when my heart feels like it will burst with pride when I watch my child sing in a school concert? What is that feeling that comes when I watch a sunset and stand in awe at the beauty? There is no concrete, definitive proof that can be offered--but these are simply examples of the soul at work. It can't be measured or quantified nor can it be observed on an x-ray or MRI scan, but it is the only truly rational explanation for those emotions, both pleasurable and not, that make the human distinct from other species. We may have a brain that sends out chemicals into the body when we experience pain or pleasure or fear, and our bodies may react accordingly, yet when push comes to shove, these physiological explanations still can't explain how those emotions can so effectively overwhelm us. Only through accepting the soul as an undeniable part of a human being can such things be understood with any clarity at all.

Return to the schools and the question as to why they should need to take into account the souls of their students. To accept this as even being possible, one first has to be willing to accept that the soul is a real and undeniable part of a human being. The second realization is that this part of the human is in need of experiencing all of those emotions that are so intertwined therein, both those things that bring us to the peaks of pleasurable feelings and those that plumb the depths and darkness of our being. Even in those moments when we experience grief or pain, the soul is making itself felt, and like those times of great joy, love or peace, both the pleasurable and painful emotions are necessary to make us whole beings. In order for these emotions to occur, we need to have the opportunities to engage in those things that bring about exercise to the soul, ensuring its health. While some of these come as a matter of course in day to day living, others are less and less likely and it seems that more and more of our fellow humans are failing to find the time for such experiences and as has been illustrated, their souls are rebelling.

While all of this is true for many people within our society, the schools are a logical place for the inclusion and maintenance of those things that nurture the soul. Since there are so many variables affecting the people in our society at large, the schools become a rational place to offer nurturance to the soul for the simple reason that it is the one place that we know the overwhelming majority of young people will experience at some point in their lives. There is no guarantee that all will have the experience of a church or synagogue or even any connection with faith at all. We cannot assume that all will come from homes where they are placed at the center of the adults' priorities. We cannot believe that they will simply find opportunities to provide for the needs of their souls on their own. Truly the only sure place for such to occur is within the classrooms of the schools we know they will have the opportunity to attend. Unlike the remainder of our society which has no common ground where the soul could be exercised and nurtured, the schools are able to provide that one constant in the lives of American youth and through that fact alone, become reasonable places for it to occur.

Unfortunately, as discussed earlier, schools are recognized for this facet of their being by a number of outside factions who call on the schools to address an entire range of real and perceived issues, thereby moving them further and further from the simple days of reading, writing and arithmetic. We can, however, still add well enough to put two and two together and realize that as these things have increased the responsibilities of the schools, there has been a corresponding decrease in other areas and upon closer inspection and with further understanding it is clear that these have been those areas that would nurture the soul. The consequence has been an increase in the number of unhappy, dissatisfied and problematic students who are attending or not attending, American schools.

I am not naive enough, nor perhaps so idealistic, to think that the schools could simply return to the "good old days"; to throw out the need to teach our students in those areas that provide them with skills in math, science and technology for their lives as future workers. Nor would I claim that schools should throw out those other outside pressures that have them checking for immunizations, addressing issues of gender and racial equity, AIDS education or whatever else they are called upon to do, for that previously identified reason that they are the best place to assure that all of America's children are reached on these issues. I am, however, fully convinced that American schools' potential to work on providing opportunities for the exercise of the souls of their students is not outside the realm of possibility. It is not something that would require one more training session or in-service, nor will it require extra time out of an already full day. Rather, it is something that will require an understanding and acceptance of the soul as an important part of a human being as real as the body and the brain and as in need of care. With this, comes the realization that in order for us to allow students to leave our schools as whole, intact beings who can effectively function in the world they enter, the soul needs to be recognized and given attention as readily as we give acknowledgement and focus to the intellect.

To risk overkill on this point, it is important to once again point out that within our schools, requirements are constantly being increased and more and more is being demanded of students. But any educator will verify that, as noted earlier, those who participate in those things that provide avenues for the development and growth of their souls as noted here generally will attain at a higher level than those who do not have access to such opportunities. It boils down to that simple truth that if students have the means to provide for exercise and strength to the soul, they are happier. Students who are happier have much less inclination to seek ways to satisfy those soul needs through drugs, alcohol, violence or any of the other means offered by the outside voices of the world. As they spend less time with the negative and more time in creating and producing those things that bring joy and contentment, the child has more time to devote to other things as well, including the intellectual. The student has been provided the means to attain a balance and that balance leads to greater satisfaction in school and in life beyond it as well.

LOOKING AT A SOULFUL FUTURE

All of the foregoing in this book has sought to offer an explanation to why we need to return to balancing the needs of our students' intellects with the needs of their souls. As with other ideas and theories for change, it is valuable to immerse ourselves in a vision, even perhaps an idealistic one, as to what would be different if that which is recommended were to occur. Because I have so often taken myself on a mind travel that allowed me to picture our schools and our world as they could be with the acknowledgement and nurturance of the human soul, I would be remiss not to offer that same travel here.

216

In moving into a world where the soul has received the focus and care that it deserves, the first thing that is noticed is that the inhabitants seem to be happier. The earlier pictures of violence, graffiti, decay, hopelessness, environmental disregard, general malaise and dissatisfaction that were so prevalent at one time have diminished. There is a slower pace and a less frenetic world. The urban blight that once left a pervading feeling of gloom has lessened. Terrifying images of random crime and violence have faded from the top stories of the news programs. The people are less likely to disregard either their environment or their fellow humans. Technological progress and gains have not stopped or gone away, but there is a balance reached so that the people are in control of them as opposed to the other way around. It is little wonder that with all these changes, the humans seem so much more content.

Within the schools of America over the past few years an understanding has been developed in the value of the soul and the need to provide it with exercise, nurture and care. Here too, things are very different than they once were. As in the society at large, the students are happier. Drop out rates are at an all time low. The thought of hallway or classroom violence or the fear that someone might bring a gun into the school is gone. Classroom disruptions have been minimized and the students seem satisfied with the progress they are making as do the teachers who instruct them. As in the society at large, the schools are so vastly different from their predecessors that a closer examination is warranted to determine how they arrived at this place.

In conducting this examination, it can be seen that the students within these schools now have a clear understanding of nature and its beauty and simplicity. They have been taught to value and appreciate the world and environment around them

217

and have come to learn the very valuable lessons that can be had there. Because they have learned these lessons well, they recognize the circular pattern found in nature at large and in life in general. For these students, the concept of "what goes around, comes around" is more than just an old adage. They realize that in the natural flow of the world they live in, anything that violates Mother Nature or human nature will not only be unsuccessful, but will cause disruption and destruction in the process. They are, therefore, less likely to go against the natural movement of the world around them and instead have learned how to blend with it. In recognizing that cyclical process of nature, they don't fight or seek to circumvent any natural process, but rather blend with it to their own advantage. In the environment around them, this means that they have a healthier concern and are more inclined to care for the world that they are inheriting. In terms of human nature, it means that they don't seek to control others through anger or violence, recognizing that in doing so they would be seeking to manage that nature through non-natural means. They know that to do anything that disrupts the natural flow of either the environment or the people around them is to seek to break a circle that is not meant to be broken.

Too, these students are much more self-reliant than they once were. Totally at ease in working in groups and understanding the value of group thought and consensus, they also recognize the importance and significance of individual thought. If they are not in agreement with the ideas or movement of a group, they feel confident in moving along their own path and following their own ideas. The ability to trust in themselves has provided other benefits as well. Because they recognize the worth of their inner voice and thoughts, they more effectively assess the voices of the world around them. Critical, accurate assessments can be made as to the merit of everything from advertised products to peer pressure tactics, and because of this, they are less likely to be swayed to the inappropriate.

Combined with their self-reliance, these students also demonstrate self-sufficiency in their ability to entertain themselves effectively and appropriately. Less time is spent in front of the television or VCR and more is devoted to natural pursuits such as drawing, painting, writing, walking in nature and taking quiet time alone to process thoughts. These opportunities allow the students to develop a complete circle through which their self-reliance leads them to pursue the positive things in life, which brings happiness, which allows them to be self-sufficient and so the circle goes. These self-reliant students have few, if any, crutches in their life and such strength brings peace of mind to these who needn't depend upon anything outside themselves for their self-worth or quality of life.

Closely interwoven with this self-reliance is the manner in which the students create. Where once a sizable number of students created in a negative fashion, it has been replaced by the positive creations of students who have had the value of art and arts-related course work reestablished into the academic day. All students have the opportunity and are strongly encouraged to find an artistic outlet during the course of their school day, thereby enhancing their access to beauty, simplicity and freedom. As they create, their work in painting, drawing, writing, singing, playing music or acting is praised, encouraged and supported. Even those students who have yet to find their best-suited area of artistic endeavor are nurtured and guided in their attempts. As the students find happiness in the strength of their self-reliance, likewise they find a pure joy and satisfaction in being able to create and have their creations acknowledged and recognized as having value. Again this perpetuates itself and another circle is formed, in this case with a resulting upswing in positive creations and a correlational decrease in inappropriate or negative ones.

All of this has led to the changes now apparent in the students. They are, in a word, balanced. They demonstrate no loss of value in the intellectual pursuit of knowledge, rather blend this with a trust in their instinct, intuition and inner voice and an understanding that there are mysteries in life not to be answered through textbooks. They maintain an appreciation for the wonders of the technological world around them but not at the expense of appreciating the wonders of the natural world. They recognize the needs of humankind to work together as a cohesive group, while appreciating and allowing for the needs, thoughts and beliefs of the individuals who comprise those groups. Because of this, they give serious critical assessment as to whether to sacrifice their own individual wants and desires to those of the group. This balance provides for healthy and whole individuals who don't feel pressured and dissatisfied by spending too much time on one side or the other of life's various streams of thoughts or behaviors. For the most part, they steer a steady, middle course that allows them to sail through the waters with a high degree of comfort, security and peace of mind.

If this is taken one step further and these students are pictured as young adults moving into the world at large, less dysfunction is found due in large part to all that has just been observed. The lessons afforded them by schools that knew enough to provide for exercise and nurture of the soul have allowed for adults who don't constantly look for satisfaction outside of themselves or place blame if life doesn't meet their expectations. They have not moved into the society with that "what if..." mentality or one that pins eventual happiness on "when" something is attained. In finding happiness and peace within themselves, they are unlikely to buy something that promises contentment, realizing that such will only offer short-term relief at best. Their satisfaction in life is found in the things that are easily had in the world around them: the beauty of nature, the simplicity of a walk in a park, the self-worth that comes through individual creation, the freedom from being owned by a mound of debt and an unsatisfying job that seeks to control that debt. Absent all those things that once caused dysfunction, these young adults now operate in a world where they are the effective contributors that society had once sought to create by training them as efficient members of the economic machinery of the world around them at the expense of their souls.

In becoming effective contributors, they have eliminated many of those problems that once prevented the society from being truly economically efficient. The decay and graffiti that once cost tax dollars for repair and removal is gone since there is value found in positive creations. Since life is no longer seen as the struggle it once was, the need to turn to drugs and alcohol for relief has declined. With its disappearance goes the expense of health care and treatment centers for rehabilitation and the cost for prison space to house the dealers. This decline has led to a like decline in violence on the streets and the need for the costly police protection that sought to control it. The value placed in nature and the environment has led to a decrease in the amount of pollution and waste that is allowed to enter America's streams, waterways and protected lands. With this, large expenditures on toxic waste clean-ups have been scaled back. Because so much money is saved in these and the other areas where we once threw dollars in an effort to stem the rising tide of problems, we're now able to use those dollars in more efficient and effective ways that better serve our world and our society as a whole.

It is not only directly in the world at large where the movement of these young adults has had an impact, but on their own personal lives and families as well. Without all the problems that once plagued so many people, these have found themselves able to avoid the dysfunction that once marked the society. They are able to create homes and families where there is love and joy and peace. The children that they raise are placed at the center of the adults' priorities and receive the love, nurture and support that they need and deserve so that their souls can develop and thrive. If this seems to be another circle in the making, perhaps that's because it is.

And so the mind travel ends. A professor in college once remarked to me that I was too much of an idealist to ever survive in the world of education and perhaps that previous little journey into fantasy proves it. On the other hand, perhaps idealism is what this world needs, since there seems so little to be found. "Idealists are people who believe in the potential of human nature for transformation..." writes M. Scott Peck. "...The most essential attribute of human nature is its mutability and freedom from instinct--that it is always within our power to change our nature. So it is actually the idealists who are on the mark and the realists who are off base."[1] Perhaps that is why I am plagued by the question as to whether a future like the one glimpsed has true potential. I can idealistically believe that we are able to change our behaviors and to heed those things that we believe are right, yet I am also enough of a realist to understand that the thoughts, beliefs, habits and behaviors that have been established over the years are deeply ingrained in our society and anything so deeply ingrained takes generations to overcome, and then only with conscientious determination. And such determination to change can't be developed unless there is a solid foundation of understanding as to why the change is necessary.

One of the buzz words heard in business, industry and education today is the term "paradigm shift", which refers to a change in the normal way of thinking to one that is dramatically different. Experts discuss how difficult a paradigm shift is to accomplish even with relevant facts and statistical data to support a given change in thought or behavior. Understanding this, the hope that American schools can undergo a huge change so as to develop means to exercise and nurture the soul, that entity without any tangible evidence of actual existence nor statistical data for support, is truly idealistic. It is not, however, beyond the scope of what is possible.

The first step in accomplishing such a paradigm shift to appreciating the value of the soul is to grant the possibility, if not the probability, of its existence. Having done this, the next step is to reflect back on those things that the soul needs for its health-- self-reliance, beauty, simplicity, creativity,love and faith--to see that there are millions of souls that are suffering due to a profound lack of these things in the world around them. When this is coupled with an examination of how we generally attempt to solve the problems and difficulties we encounter as we move through life, we see more neglect to the soul. The beauty of nature is lost as we sacrifice more forests to the needs of the housing and construction industries and dump our waste into streams and rivers. Simplicity loses out to the growing complexity arising from everything from family dysfunction to modern technological advances. Our fast-paced, hectic society and our desire to keep up with others precludes us from opportunities to engage in positive, enjoyable and soul-nurturing creations. The growth in the industry that provides places to lay blame for our misfortunes has destroyed our self-reliance and has left us weak, afraid and wallowing in hardship. And with all of this, our focus on all of those things that are difficult, wrong or unpleasant about this world we live in has left us with less time to enjoy the connection, friendship and love of the people around us. In considering all this, there is little wonder that the neglect of the soul is making itself known in so many people in so many ways and is contributing to the formation of a vicious circle that perpetuates all of the hardship we see around us.

There are few people who would disagree with the idea that something needs to change. The variety of initiatives being promoted by government and the private sector for environmental clean-ups, improved health care, welfare reform, crime prevention, strengthening of the family and the like speak to a wide-spread recognition that there is a great need for change if our society is to remain a viable one in the years to come. Yet a teacher of mine once wisely advised breaking things down to their most basic level in order to determine their true worth. As this is done with the various reforms and initiatives being touted today, at that most basic level they appear to do nothing more than add additional complexity to a world already too bogged down in it. As well, despite the best intentions of the government or private sector, it is unlikely that any truly bold initiative that could feasibly impact the majority of American citizens in a soul-nurturing, positive way will make it through all of the bureaucracy and in-fighting and remain unchanged. More likely, it would end up as a watered-down version, barely resembling its original form and with little potential for impact.

So we return again to the schools and the potential for

change there, not only in the manner in which our young people are educated, but also in the end results of such change. Having accepted the existence of the soul as, at the very least, a possibility and having developed an understanding of what it is that the soul needs in order to allow for a happy and whole individual, those responsible for the education of American students have completed the first step in their paradigm shift. From there, educators need to critically assess the program that they are providing at the level that they teach. Is certain material being included in the curriculum that would be more developmentally appropriate later on in the child's education or life? As educators, have we become so infatuated with the ever-improving technology that we are not critically assessing how much background a student needs in that area during their years in a K-12 system? Are the times for recess, art, music and physical education gradually being decreased to make way for more work in math, science, technology and work-related skill development? Are graduation requirements so strenuous that the average and below-average student will have no time for aesthetically pleasing and enjoyable pursuits? Do all of the students feel loved, accepted and cared for by the entire adult staff in the building? Is it possible that all of the improvements that have been made in teaching to the intellect have allowed for an unintended, yet total disregard for the whole child? Is there an even-handed approach in the way we educate our young or have we lost any balance? And if so, how do we regain it?

An honest assessment of these and related questions if truly answered by the majority of educators in American schools would yield an overwhelming consensus that we have, indeed, lost balance and that we currently teach almost solely to the intellect. The consensus would also be that these seem to be very dark days in public education due to the problems, hardships and dysfunction being brought into the classrooms every day. They would speak of restructuring, cooperative learning, technological improvements, lengthened school days and any number of other reforms implemented to allow students to learn more or which seek to alleviate problems, but they would further admit that all of these have done little.

What they haven't done is remembered the soul. It just seems too simplistic and I would venture to guess that in few schools or classrooms across America has anyone dared to suggest that many of the difficulties being experienced might just be due to the neglect of the souls of the students. It would be almost heretical for an educator to suggest that perhaps all those noted improvements, viewed by the majority as so beneficial for students may well be one of the things creating and reinforcing the problems. Yet nature does teach valuable lessons and one of those lessons is well-remembered here. In all of Creation, when the balance of nature is thrown off kilter, it invariably seeks to restore its equilibrium. Likewise, when the balance of life is thrown out of kilter for those young people in our charge, equilibrium will naturally be sought. Either we will find ways to provide this balance for them, or they will continue to seek it for themselves in ways that are detrimental and damaging not only to themselves, but also to the schools and the world around them. Yet we hesitate to do this. In reality though, if providing such balance is as basic as utilizing our wisdom and abilities to provide opportunities for students to find the beauty, freedom, simplicity, creativity, self-reliance, love and faith so needed by the soul and potentially so easily had in the schools they attend, what is the worst that could happen? And having answered that question to your satisfaction, what is the best that could happen? If you have trouble with that one, you need only return to that shared mind travel of a few paragraphs ago.

Even lacking a total change in the movement of education, it is very possible for individual teachers, administrators, parents and other adults to become cognizant of the soul needs of children and either begin providing or working to maintain those things that will offer nurturance to the soul. Within classrooms, whether in math and science, the arts, or any other area, individual teachers can provide avenues for children to have time during which they create products wholly on their own, without the aid of computers or technology. They can be offered the opportunity to rely on their instincts and intuitions in the completion of a drawing or painting or story which illustrates a concept being studied. Teachers can operate with a degree of academic freedom and latitude in determining how much time during the course of a day or week students are taught work-place competencies and how much time will be devoted to pursuits that are valuable solely because of their creative, soul-nurturing potentials. Administrators and counselors can work more effectively in helping students they work with find value in the things that they are being asked to do and can likewise encourage their teachers to achieve a balance between intellectual skills and the creative realm. Parents and others can seek ways to encourage children to take time alone, away from the television or home computer, to think and reflect and to draw on their inner resources for enjoyment and relaxation. And all adults who impact children can remember what it is to be a child and how important it is to take small steps that are neither impeded nor rushed. In doing so, the adults may realize that the soulfulness that is so much a part of being a child is a valuable commodity that we don't want to do away with, but encourage, nurture and maintain so as to enable our children to become adults who are truly effective and efficient members of the society they will enter.

A good friend of mine talks about the need for the pendulum of humankind to swing from one extreme to the other in order to find the center.   As we reflect on our emphasis in teaching to the spiritual and inner needs of the young during the early period in our history as opposed to the stress and importance placed on teaching to the intellect today, it is very clear that the pendulum has truly swung from those extremes.   Idealistic though it may be, it seems logical that we now move to a time when we find a balance between these two, recognizing that no human can live happily when one part of his being is nurtured at the expense of another.   In doing so, we will be better equipped to nurture more than just the minds and bodies of the students within our schools, and will as well begin our work in rediscovering and caring for the lost souls in American education.

———————

REFERENCES

INTRODUCTION:

1. Robert Sardello, Love and the Soul: Creating a Future for Earth; (New York: HarperCollins Publishers, Inc. 1995) p. xiv.
2. Thomas Moore, Care of the Soul: A Guide for Cultivating Depth and Sacredness in Everyday Life; (New York: HarperCollins Publishers, Inc. 1992) p.5.

CHAPTER 1:

1. Ralph Waldo Emerson, "Self-Reliance", Selected Essays, Lectures and Poems, Robert E. Spiller, Ed. (New York: Simon and Schuster, 1975) p.245.
2. C.G. Jung, Modern Man in Search of a Soul; (Orlando, FL: Harcourt Brace Jovanovich, Publishers 1933) p. 185.
3. Robert Sardello, Love and the Soul: Creating a Future for Earth; (New York: HarperCollins Publishers, Inc. 1995) p.xvii.
4. Thomas Moore, Care of the Soul: A Guide for Cultivating Depth and Sacredness in Everyday Life; (New York: HarperCollins Publishers, Inc. 1992) p. xi.
5. C.G. Jung, Modern Man in Search of a Soul; (Orlando, FL: Harcourt Brace Jovanovich Publishers 1933) pg. 239.
6. D.P. Gardner and Y.W. Larsen, "A Nation at Risk," National Commision on Excellence in Education, U.S. Department of Education, 1983.
7. Congressional Digest, January 1994, pg. 11.

CHAPTER 2:

1. Benjamin Hoff, The Te of Piglet, (New York: Penguin Books USA, Inc. 1992) p. 71.
2. Thomas Moore, Care of the Soul: A Guide for Cultivating Depth and Sacredness in Everyday Life, (New York: HarperCollins Publishers, Inc. 1992) p. 52.
3. Benjamin Hoff, The Te of Piglet, (New York: Penguin Books USA, Inc. 1992) pp. 72-73.

4. "Great Transitions: Preparing Adolescents for a New Century": The Carnegie Council on Adolescent Development, 1995.

PART II:

1. James A. Johnson, Harold W. Collins, Victor L. Dupuis, John H. Johansen., Introduction to the Foundations of American Education, (Newton, MA: Allyn and Bacon, 1985) p.275.

CHAPTER 3:

1. Aldous Huxley, Brave New World, (New York: Harper Collins Publishers, 1946) p. 28.
2. Ralph Waldo Emerson, "Self-Reliance", Selected Essays, Lectures and Poems, Robert E. Spiller, Ed. (New York: Simon and Schuster, 1975) p. 253.

CHAPTER 4:

1. C.G. Jung, Modern Man in Search of a Soul, (Orlando, FL: Harcourt Brace Jovanovich Publishers, 1933) p. 238.
2. Ibid., p.234.
3. Ibid., p. 234.

CHAPTER 5:

1. Gerald W. Grumet, M.D., as cited in "Quotable Quotes", Readers Digest, July, 1995, pg. 161.
2. Benjamin Hoff, The Te of Piglet, (New York: Penguin Books USA, Inc. 1992) pp. 71-72.

CHAPTER 7:

1. Ralph Waldo Emerson, "Beauty", Selected Essays, Lectures and Poems, Robert E. Spiller, Ed. (New York: Simon and Schuster, 1975) pp. 185-186.

CHAPTER 8:

1. C. G. Jung, Modern Man in Search of a Soul, (Orlando, FL: Harcourt Brace Jovanovich Publishers, 1933) p.165.

CHAPTER 9:

1. M. Scott Peck, Further Along the Road Less Traveled, (New York: Simon and Schuster, 1993) pp.35-36.

Chapter 10:

1. M. Scott Peck, People of the Lie: The Hope for Healing Human Evil, (New York: Simon and Schuster, 1983) p. 247.